First published in South Africa 2012 by

BrandBabes@Work Entertainments Corporation.

Address at 25 Faraday Boulevard

Central West 1

Vanderbijl Park

1911

Gauteng

South Africa

Given the rights to publish to Smashwords.com in its capacity as a publisher of digital and electronic media, by Coty Mampeule in his capacity as the author and the director and owner of BrandBabes@Work Entertainments Corporation. South Africa

Disclaimer:

In this work of fiction, the characters, places and events are either the product of the author's imagination or they are used entirely fictitiously.

Any reference to any person or business whether living or dead is purely coincidental.

The authors shall accept no liability in case such is recognized.

Welcome to My Dream Is My Key

Chapter 1

My Dream Is My Key is a phenomenon derived from studying the Fafi game of bets, mostly played in South Africa by township women since the early days of Apartheid era. It intertwines the symbols used in Fafi to help people to have a guideline to bigger betting games such as Lotteries, Horse-Races and other known game of chance. Although it attempts to guide you to select your betting numbers using the stated methods, it does not serve as a guarantee to have you winning the game of whatever it is you are betting for. It serves to eliminate the loss of your money by clearly understanding where the author is coming from, using his methods by his way of observation and the self study that he has conducted while writing this book. Treat this as a fun way of choosing your numbers by listening and noting your dreams. Gambling is about fun and while you are having fun, you should win yourself a lot and lots of huge bucks.

The author attempts to write it in a simpler and a great way to understand it and use the methods in a clear uncomplicated manner. The English will be simple even for people who are not much literate in English so that they understand the methods used for fun and lots of winning opportunities. Some rules noted can be bent as there's no tried and tested method of winning any game of chance, but we intend to reduce time it takes you to waste money by just placing your bets without firstly checking what other avenues may be around you, to carefully listening to what your Dreams are Really telling you, and placing your bets in an educated way.

We have tried to check which sites on the net, that can teach and show you methods of Dreams Interpretations to a direct Numbers selection for betting purposes, and we struggled a bit. We hope this is your answer to your quest as no South African has tried (as far as we know), to share this great methods used for so many years. You will be amazed by how much your dreams are made of binary systems like that used by a computer as its language. The Dreams mostly come in an analogue rather than digital system, where we try to digitalize your dreams and convert them into numbers.

Let's Have Some Fun...

History of Fa-Fi

We have read the Wikipedia definition and history noted, and we can't say it less than the truth, as we can only observe that most of the information matches what we know. If we were given a chance to write the history ourselves, we would not deviate much to what it is written in Wikipedia page except that we will carry on to expand to greater heights on the matter, based on the personal experience. The trouble with that, is, we would depend on other people's personal experiences too, to match our own to authenticate the reality on the matter to the story or the history.

This is how the Wikipedia describes the Definition...

Fafi or *fa-fi* (pronounced Faah-Feeh), also known as mo-china, is a form of betting played mainly by black South African women, particularly those living in South African Townships and is believed to have originated with South Africa's Chinese community. This game can also be linked to the Italian Lottery which is also called the Number Racket.

Playing Fafi

Fafi participants choose the number they want to gamble on by interpreting their dreams. This dream interpretation or conversion is based upon a variety of systems. When they have decided upon their lucky number, participants will then place a bet on their number. A dream about robbers (izigebengu/amasela) may indicate the number 7. A dream about a white person (umLungu) is the number 3, whereas a dream about the sea could either indicate the number 18 for a ship (inqanawe) or 26, the number for water (amanzi).

The game requires a woman runner (isikhwama - bag) to take a bag of bets, along with the names of the betters and their money, to someone, usually Chinese, who visits the station (house) of the runner holding the betting session. The Chinese person will take the bag from the runner and then whisper the winning number to her. The runner will then indicate with her hands to the betters which number has won, and that person will be paid out.

 "Mo-China" as it is popularly known in the townships, is the only number game that has flourished in South African townships over many years despite being illegal. As the name implies it was brought into the country by Chinese people. The following is just a hint on how this number-betting game is played. It is composed of numbers from 1 to 36 and each number has a name or character. The draw takes place twice a day i.e. morning and afternoon. For every draw only one number is chosen.

Rules of Fa-Fi

The Mo-China is supposed to draw only one Number per visit. The Number is drawn and shown (or told) to the Runner. The Runner then will show by a way signs, to tell the others what number has been selected. Immediately, people know they won. The Runner has her share of the Bag. It is paid by a certain percentage as agreed between herself and the M'China.

The Chain Reaction of Events

It is quite straight forward with no Surprises. Very transparent this game is, and trusted by millions of the women in South Africa.

However, we have to point out the Golden Rule, which is the basis of our System, which the Book and methods are derived from: The M'China can select numbers following a system of Parity. All people who place bets, are aware of what Number is the Opening Number and what Number is a Closing Number. To put it in precise simple English, the M'China cannot select a Number out of Range of the Morning, or the afternoon and even the Evening Range. We shall explain the Ranges or Parity system that rules the game.

The Parity System is the real reason that makes this game to be predictable and we came to notice through an Intensive Lottery Ten Year Self Study (2000-2010) that somehow, both games are similar in pattern.

Fa-Fi, as explained earlier, is based on a 1/36 system. As most Lotteries are based on 6/45 or 6/49 system, Fa-Fi is based on much tough selection, but people who has studied it, are able to predict their numbers correctly or just miss out by misplacing bets wrongly.

For an example, a person can study the numbers drawn throughout the day, then check what number is drawn the next morning, and then out of that number, she can start to check the Parity system and will predict the numbers for the afternoon draw. Say she predicts the number 8, and the Parity system favors the number 8, but the M'China draws the number 3. By way of the Parity system, the number 8 is the right number to select but 3 was the selected, as there would be 23 other legible numbers to select from. The 3 and 8 Parity system or rule will have 11 numbers that should not be selected at all.

This, we have dubbed a rule of the universe or simply The Universal Rule. Later we will show you how 1 and 36 Parity Rule is more like a Moon to the Earth. As the Earth has billion of stars, they are most visible in intervals according to the Earth's Rotation around the Sun, even their position will depend on the day of the year.

Later, we will also show you, in details, how to use this Parity system to place your selection for

Lotto or Power-Ball, using your sketched draws and/or your Dreams.

To explain in a schematic presentation, here is what the gambler would use.

Guideline Tools

- Number Chart

This is a chart more like previous draws chart, where she would write all the numbers drawn by date and time. This helps her to check what numbers are HOT under What Parity Rule. Like Lotto system, Fa-Fi has HOT and COLD numbers.

- Numbers Drawn

These are placed on the Number Chart

- Parity Rules (or systems)

There are 25 Parity Rules. This is from The Alpha Rule or the Moon Rule (1 and 36) to the Omega Rule (28 and 30).

- Previous Draws

This has been emphasized twice in the topics above. This helps her to make her final selection and place her numbers with a greater chance of getting to the correct prediction.

- Dreams Consultation.

This is the most fun and yet tricky thing to do. It takes practice and patience. Normally, an ardent gambler, would spend at least 2 hours placing her bets, trying to eliminate all the trivial numbers and stick to the closer to the target numbers, if that would make sense to anyone.

For her to get much greater help, she would consult one of the Astronomical helper:

Her Dreams.

Dreaming of a **Con-man** or a **Lion**, or a **Big Stick** or **Live Chicken** would convince her to place the number **7** and yet, the number has a partner which is **13**. Now if the parity system has started with the number 13, then definitely she knows her dreams are not wrong and she would take 7 as her number. The M'China may not select 7, but it is the most eligible number to be drawn. Now, she would consult her dream chart and would look at all the numbers that would support her dream number. Finally she would make her selection.

The Universal Rule

Although, very much debatable, the Fa-Fi adheres to the rule of the UNIVERSE.

- Number 1 to 36 represents
  - the Perfect Cycle or
  - The Orbit of the Earth on its own axis
  - The Revolution of the Earth around the Sun or
  - 0 degrees to the 360 degrees.
- The Parity Systems depicts the Rule in which some of the elements or Celestial Bodies are prone to laws, where they have to adhere to rules and guidelines as per the Master's Plan.
  - When the Sun shines, the Stars are not visible (Parity 2 and 29 to Parity 28 and 30)
  - When the Sun shines the Moon can still be visible in the sky (The Moon Rule or Parity Rule 1 and 36)
  - The Earth's movement and speed is constant throughout and the comets and other known celestial bodies can come closer but respect the Earth's Space, not to enter into it.

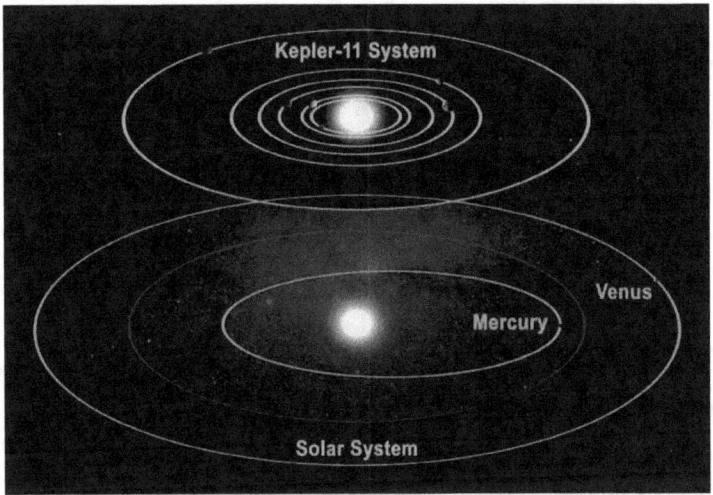

Dreams, Symbols and Numbering

Chapter 2

In this chapter, we are not going to try and be "Robert Langdon "from the Da Vinci's Code book or movie, no, but we are going to show you the ingenious way the South Africans women have succeeded to derive Numbers from Dreams and Use them and help them to Interpret their dreams for game of chance purposes. It is one of the most fascinating methods ever. We spent quiet a number of attempts to find this information on the net, but regrettably, we couldn't find even one. The closet we came was one site which interpreted the dreams into numbers but didn't show you the method. What's the point in that, one would ask. Are we that less intelligent that we cannot be shown how some systems work. With us, there are no secrets. We bear it all. Less talk more action...

Dreams

To explain what a dream is, would virtually be an ignorance that we show from our side towards our readers. Although I have not experienced an Alien Sighting, but I am sure if I would try and explain to one, that earthlings dream ... I would seriously get smacked very hard with some quantum leap hot clap for just trying to explain what a dream is.

Dreams come in many forms. I am a member of a site called Dream Moods and the site shows you so many kinds of dreams, it is so fascinating. Our quest here is not to study different dreams and what they may be saying to you, where your health or life or future or bad luck is concerned. We are more concerned about teaching how to interpret them using a method from the My Dream Is My Key.

We will show you how to use the Fa-Fi system, the Interpretation, the Wheel of Fortune and the Parity Rule to write your Lotto and Power-Ball Number Selection.

Let's take a dream example

...you go to the fridge and open it, and then you take out some Pork (8) Ribs (11) out and put them on a Dish (45 also 9). You try to pull a piece to taste, but decide to use a Small Knife (15). Then you take some Eggs (10) and boil them. You wipe the fat from the ribs with your Handkerchief (20)."

Your Lotto or Power-Ball Selection would be 8, 9, 10, 11, 15 and 20.

Symbols and Numbers

This is the crux of the matter, if you don't understand this bit, please try and get some rest and come back to this chapter.

- Fa-fi uses a 1/36 system. You select 1 one out of a group of thirty six
- Most Lotteries use a 6/45 systems. You select 6 numbers out of a group of 45.
- Some Power-Ball uses a 5/45 1/20 system. You select the first 5 numbers and then the Power-Ball out of a group of 20 numbers.

Whatever system they present themselves, they follow one rule: ***The Universal Law of Planets.***

Numbers and Symbols

1

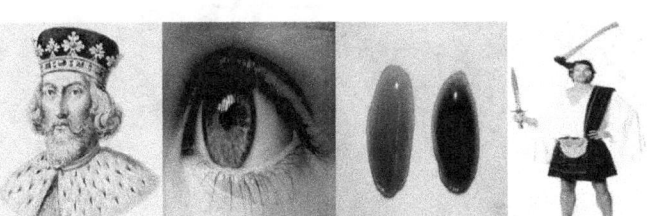

...

- *King*
- *Left Eye*
- *Blood*
- *Whiteman*

A white man is actually a white man, but if you are Caucasian, there's no way that you can take the number 1 as serious because most of your dreams would be filled with your own kind. But if another person of a different race has a dream of a white man, the number 1 would be significant. Check the number 2, 8 and 30, if you are already feeling uneasy.

Also, a King shouldn't be a Real King, but someone Superior, like your Boss, your Supervisor, your Manager Etc, or King James or Jesus.

Numbers and Symbols

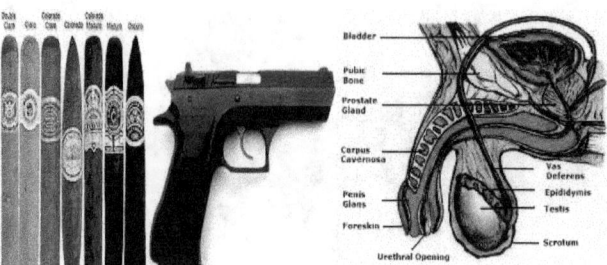

- *Cigar*
- *Gun*
- *Any Oblong Shaped Object*
- *Penis*

A frankfurter can be taken into consideration, a Vienna also. But a Base ball bet is rather a big stick than an oblong shaped object.

Numbers and Symbols

- *Monkey*
- *Money*
- *Jockey*
- *Blackman*
- *Driver*

You will note that numbers have a stipulated symbol or character and other associate characters. A black man shouldn't be too particular as he would be dreaming mostly of black people of course.

Money can be mentioned in a dream or be seen. Most of the time, when money is mentioned, the number 2 is used, but when seen, you establish the Parity Rule and/ or consider whether it is notes or coins. If coins, 18 would be the correct number and notes are seen to be a number 32.

Numbers and Symbols

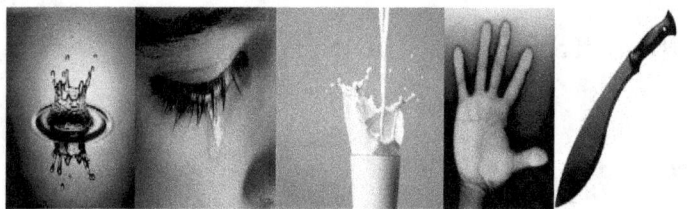

- *Small Water*
- *Tears*
- *Right Hand*
- *Milk*

- *Big Knife*

Quite clearly, you get the picture here. You don't need to scratch your head until it is no more. When you open a faucet and you drink out of it, that is what we meant by small water. And when you see tears or a carton of milk, it's what the dream is telling you.

A dream cannot tell you to look specifically for which hand you should consider, but if your dream is about that specific hand, your subconscious will make you aware of it. A big knife can be a machete or a chef's knife. Look, you shouldn't be worried about the small insignificant things about the interpretation and conversion, but your sixth sense whether strong or weak, will guide you automatically. With good practice, you will soon be able to do this like it's your second nature.

Numbers and Symbols

- **Big Water**
- **Accident**
- **Frog**
- **Sex**

Let's clear the Sea Water.

An Ocean, a Lake, a Pond, a Dam, all of these falls under Big Water.

Sex should be vivid in a dream and not just a mere mention of the word. You need to be involved in it or see other symbols be involved in it. Trying to have sex is also good enough.

Numbers and Symbols

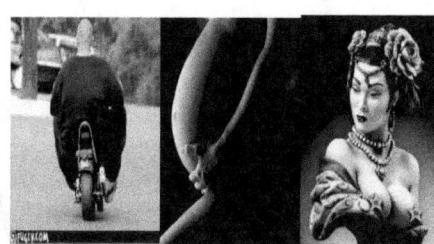

- Pig
- Drunkard
- Stout Person
- Pregnant Person
- Chinese

A Chinese can either be a male or female. But if you are a Chinese, this number wouldn't be applicable to you since most of your human symbols will be Chinese in your dream.

A Drunkard is sometimes tricky...either you see a person who you know as a Drunkard being very sober. The challenge would be how to interpret, but I would advise you to check where you are in a dream. Are you in club, are you in partying environment? That will give you a lee-way.

Numbers and Symbols

- Dead Man
- Bed
- Bee
- Turkey
- Fortune

A Dead Man has to be a Male not otherwise. There's a number for a Dead Woman.

Also a fortune will depend on your financial situation at the time of your dream. If someone gives you a cheque of $1 000 000, that would a fortune to someone who is not a Millionaire, but to a wealthy person, that's just money.

Numbers and Symbols

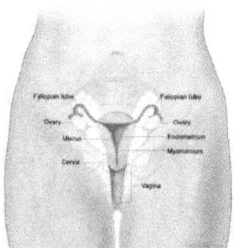

- *Big Hole*
- *Grave*
- *Hollow Things*
- *Vagina (I love the way they describe it in another language. They call it KATAPANI)*

Hollow Things could be a...

- boot of a car,
- Empty Box,
- a Ditch or
- Sewer manhole.

.

Numbers and Symbols

15

- *Prostitute (or someone behaving as such)*
- *White Horse*
- *Small Knife*

Interesting enough, a Prostitute sleeps with everyone, a White Horse is one horse everyone wants to ride, and a small knife can be in anyone's pocket. Get the picture?

Let's look at the Connecticut Classic Lotto Results on the 4th November 2011

16 Connecticut – Classic Lotto   4 Nov 2011   4,6,7,8,15,17 Payout

The Dream and Numbers:

You see a Gentleman (6) who has quite a fortune (4) who somehow, has married a crooked (7) Lady (17), who sometimes behaves like a whore (15) when drunk (8).

In a Dream, you may have observed the woman's behavior and it must have been quite palpable.

Numbers and Symbols

16

- *Clothes*
- *Dove*
- *Animal Ears*
- *Ship*
- *Small House*
- *Flag*
- *Money*

A Small House is a Toilet, a Lighthouse, Security Booth, and or Telephone Booth.

Money shows up here again exactly like in number 2. Use it interchanging to secure Parity Law depending on which direction the Lotto or Power Ball is taking.

Numbers and Symbols

- *Tiger (not in the Woods)*
- *Fight*
- *Muscular Or Strong Man*

These are clear cut symbols.

But an Argument is a form of Fight, and generally a bossy person is also a Tiger, or just showing his/her Masculine side

Numbers and Symbols

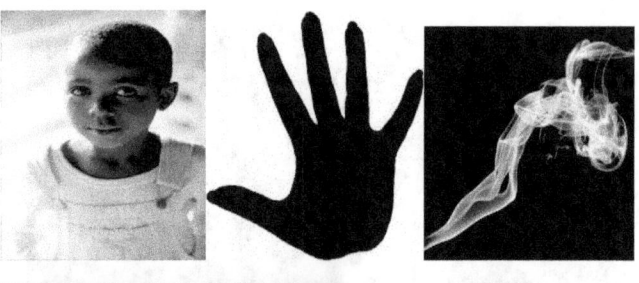

19

- *Young Girl/s*
- *Left Hand*
- *Smoke*
- *Bird*
- *Bread*

Please see Number 29 for tips on hands. Smoke can be that from cigar or a building on fire. It is clear to you that you will seek for a dream with Fire associated with it, and remember you guidance is the Parity System

Numbers and Symbols

- *Cow*
- *Gentleman*

Look at how the Number 6 shows a bovine characteristic. Gentlemen are usually and seriously gentle, so are cows.

Let's look at the example below from the New York Sweet Million Lotto Results.

40 ▤ New York - Sweet Million Lotto   7 Nov 2011 2,6,17,23,35,37 Payout

...you are lured by the charm of this Gentleman (6) and (17) who promises you Money (2). They invite you to their House (23) and you go with a smile on your face. On arrival, you notice the house is huge but very Hollow (35). You notice there's Blood (01) on the floor and you run out of the house.

Numbers and Symbols

- *Young Boy/s*
- *Toys*
- *Clouds*
- *Plane*
- *Spider*

Question!

Would you consider a Helicopter part of the symbols?

A grown person can have a dream of their son who is 40. That is a young boy to you. That is how the beauty of interpretation and practice comes in; it forces to use your intellect.

Numbers and Symbols

- *Con-Man*
- *Lion*
- *Big Stick*
- *Chicken*

This number is very tricky in its purest form. You will sometimes see a person who is a saint being sinister in your dream, and you would not know whether you should use the number 6 or 7. Thugs, killers, looters, and all ill-mannered of societal injustice persons would fall into this number. Not only that it is tricky, it can present itself in a dream and your interpretation can be taken to disarray. I'd be careful if I were you when I am doing my conversion when the number 7 is presented.

Numbers and Symbols

- *Big Fish*
- *Ghost*
- *Tail*

No wonder it pairs with the trickiest number 7. Mostly number is considered unlucky but it pairs with the luckiest number, which by definition, is also full of surprises.

Your dream can be of a humble dead man who all of a sudden tries to choke you. That would qualify him as a Ghost because of the action, but if he doesn't attack, it is just a dead man or a gentleman. The number thirteen will mislead you to use number 4 unnecessarily. Then again you may be compelled to use 4 and 13 which in most Parity Rules takes the number 15 and 35.

Here is another one, a Tail. A detective could b tailing your activities or you may see a tail light of a thunderbird car. You would be lucky if you just dream of a tail of a Big Fish you just caught knocking you into the water.

Numbers and Symbols

- *Moon*
- *Owl*
- *Hat*
- *Baby*
- *Lamp*
- *Dish*
- *Pumpkin*

Number 9 is busy with symbols, but I want concentrate on the Dish and Baby. A Dish can be a cooked meal on a Dish or just Dishes in a sink.

A baby can be a young of an animal, bird or human being. But there's a number for a newborn. When you see a Baby in your dream, it doesn't matter whether it's a boy or a girl, because if you come to think of it, when they are young, we struggle to tell if they are boys or girls.

Numbers and Symbols

17

- *Diamond/s*
- *Lady*
- *Queen*
- *White Woman*

I know you are beginning to wonder why a White Woman. In the Pre-1994 era in South Africa, white women were considered to be beautiful and if a young black lady would apply makeup and wear a lipstick, they would be considered fashionable and yet Slutty. And because it was social taboo for a young black man to talk to a white woman, a dream of a white woman would be considered a BAD DREAM. Back in the days, white South African Women, would be disgusted to be approached by a black guy for friendship endeavors. They would be seen as people who consider themselves as Queens and loved Gold, Money, and Diamonds. You would be astonished by how many times 2, 3, 32 numbers and 16 match your number 17 in your dream. This one I have seen with most dreams I try to interpret whether mine or through the Lotto Results I do on my blog page. On another note, the Fa-Fi dreams symbols do not have a number for other races females but only 17. So it safe to say, when a Caucasian male dream of a white woman, he would by the nature of his surrounding, dream of a white woman, but if you are a African American or an Asian and you dream of a white woman, you would want to note the number 17 in your selection. Though times have changed since Nelson Mandela changed all of the laws of Apartheid, a dream of a white woman, is still considered as a Bad Dream by South African households.

Numbers and Symbols

- *Egg/s*
- *Ball*
- *Train*
- *Round Object*

Round objects include

- Oranges,
- Apples,
- Tires,
- Globes,

You dream you are in Rainy weather (18) fishing (21: a fisherman). You are surprised (28) to catch a Tiger (5) shark. When you cut open it with a small knife (15), you see it had some Eggs (10) about to leave its body.

Numbers and Symbols

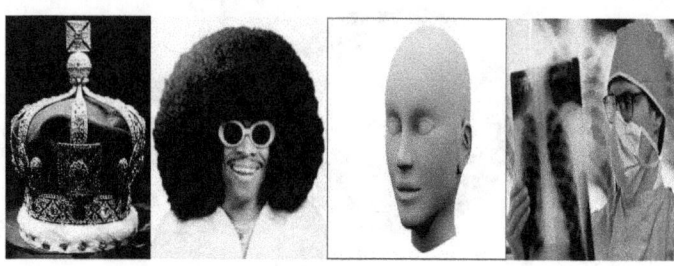

- *House*
- *Crown*
- *Hair*
- *Head*
- *Doctor*

A Head of Department is not 23, but 1. A head has to be a head in a true sense of a word.

A house would be

- a dog kennel,
- an apartment,
- A regular sized house.

A castle, a skyscraper, a mansion or as school would have its own number.

Numbers and Symbols

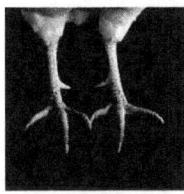 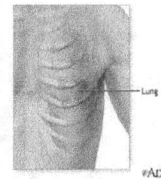  

- *Chicken Feet*
- *Car*
- *Ribs*

The First two are quite straight forward but Ribs are quite tricky but not a tricky as 7 is.

Pork Ribs would have two numbers (8) and (11).

Please look carefully at the word Pork (pig) and Ribs. You may skip ribs and go for pig here unaware. If your dream includes someone in a fatal accident and his Rib cage has been badly fractured, the number 11 is the right selection.

Look at this example

47 South Africa - Powerball   8 Nov 2011 8,10,11,15,45 20 Payout

---

...you go to the fridge and open it, and then you take out some Pork (8) Ribs (11) out and put them on a Dish (45 also 9). You try to pull a piece to taste, but decide to use a Small Knife (15). Then you take some Eggs (10) and boil them. You wipe the fat from the ribs with your Handkerchief (20)."

Numbers and Symbols

- *Funeral*
- *Bees*
- *Bush*
- *Mad Person*

59 U.S.A. - Mega Millions   4 Nov 2011 26,30,32,33,44 1 Payout

Mega Dreams for Mega Millions...These are big numbers here. I bet the dream is sweet also.

You are attending a Funeral (26) where a Fat (44 also 8) Priest (30) is preaching. Suddenly a very Drunk (8) Ill-mannered wife (32) starts to sob uncontrollably, saying her King (1) is dead. This had some Young Boy (33) giggling.

Numbers and Symbols

- **Dead Woman**
- **Chinese**
- **Queen**
- **Fire**

Please note how some symbols repeat themselves, like queen, and Chinese. You may be tempted to dismiss other symbols and would want to stick to other numbers instead, but if your dream is about a Queen, and the Parity Rule doesn't favor 17, your quick remedy is the number 12. Or if the Parity doesn't favor the number 8, then you opt for the number 12. Interesting isn't it?

A dead woman has to be strictly a dead woman and not a dead body.

Question!

Is your late Grandma a dead woman or just an Old Woman?

Numbers and Symbols

- *Paper Money (Notes)*
- *Gold nuggets or Bar*
- *Snake*
- *Ill-mannered Woman*

I want to draw your attention to the last symbol.

This is a loud mouthed, blasphemous woman, who can curse, cheat, connive, lure, lust, and backstab. The character doesn't have to be confused with 15 as slutty, but if she shows up as half naked or flashing her number 35, then you are in luck to have 35 and 32 as your numbers.

A woman, who treats kids' slaves in a dream, would fit this character, or just a disrespectful woman to a husband or any person befitting to be considered a number 6.

Numbers and Symbols

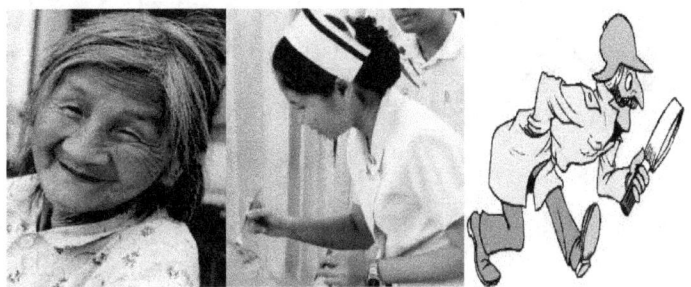

- *Old Woman*
- *Nurse*
- *Detective*

This is a tricky one for me most of the time when I see my mother in my dream. Although she is both a Nurse and Old, I seem to struggle to place in a situation where I see her and my brother in one dream. My brother is quite a Gentleman who can also portray a character of being devious. I struggle to place him as 23 (Doctor) or 7 (Con-man), but I am quick to consult my number chart for Parity Rules and System check.

Numbers and Symbols

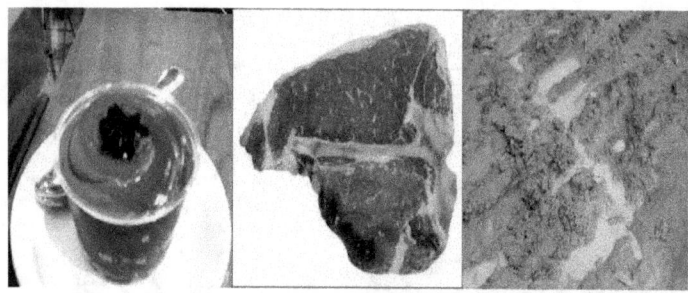

- *Faeces or Defecation (Or Doing number two, as it is widely known is South Africa)*
- *Dirty Objects*
- *Pudding*
- *Mud*
- *Meat*

Dirty objects can include anything that attracts bad smell or odor, but MEAT should be any meat whether rotten or not.

Question!

Would kneading dough for pizza considered as 34? Apply your mind!

I encourage you to use Wheel of Fortune and Parity System, know it by heart and recite it if possible, to align yourself to a quicker understanding of the dreams interpretations. If you are not much of a fun gambling person, you'd find all of this useless, but getting richer is everyone's dream and wishes.

Numbers and Symbols

- *Coins (or loose change)*
- *Right Eye*
- *Chain*
- *Belt*
- *Rain*
- *Butterfly*

I earlier mentioned the specific of Money in your dream and I will re-iterate. Paper Money is 32 and Coins is 18 but Money in general is 2.

How do you see if it's a Right Eye of Left Eye in a dream? Consider the direction of what you see and which side it is. When you turn left, your left eye is the one to notice the said sight, peripherally.

Numbers and Symbols

- *Fire*
- *Feather*
- *Lipstick*
- *Horse Shoe*
- *Bishop*
- *Excitement*

You dream of a Pope standing next to a Bishop and a Priest. What number would you consider here? In fact is it one, two or three numbers? The Pope is more like a King, a Bishop is number 31 and a Priest is another number still to be discussed. Try and free your mind and *the more you practice, the luckier you will get.*

Numbers and Symbols

- *Cat*
- *Music*
- *Paymaster*
- *Driver*
- *Nude Woman*
- *Handkerchief*

Remember that number 2 is also a Driver. This is where you have options to derive your own skill when you use the Parity System and the Universal rule.

Numbers and Symbols

- *Big House*
- *Boxer*

A castle, a skyscraper, a mansion or as school would have its own number. This is what I said earlier, under number 23.

A Boxer is a kind of a dog and also an athletic type of sportsman. Which one is considered here? You are absolutely right, an athletic sportsmen who beat each other mercilessly, wrecking their brains for the love of showing off and money, and not a dog.

But I love the sport. I tried it and didn't like it. I guess the other guy was angrier than I was. I ended kicking him in the groin out of frustration. I couldn't take that much beating and it's all because of the fact that I wanted to change from being a karate person to a boxing person. Also I was not pleased with the fact that you can't block the punch by swerving it away but rather duck, which had me so much frustrated that I kicked the guy in the groin with a mai Geri kick and administered a nice spinning mawasha Geri on his temple before I surrendered my gloves. Then I tried kick boxing and still the first person who I sparred with was much tougher and older. Him, I had the pleasure of breaking his nose with my forehead, and I was told that I use my head, but that I knew, I couldn't take the punishments.

When my mother saw me with the black eyes, she administered a beating much worse than that I got from the 15 year old kick boxer, as I was only 11.

Hey back to business.

Numbers and Symbols

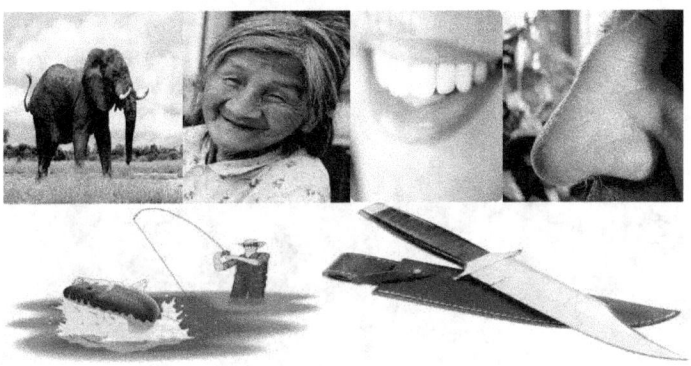

- *Elephant*
- *Old Woman*
- *Teeth*
- *Nose*
- *Fisherman*
- *Knife*

A knife is shown here again, and also 13 is but a big knife. Obviously this would be your middle sized knife.

Also note an old woman. Once again an advantage to place your numbers and dreams to favor your selection, but the idea is to try and match the numbers.

Teeth could be a result of a smile or anger or a bite. Example is that of a shark biting someone's left leg. 13, 22 and 21 would be the right numbers.

Numbers and Symbols

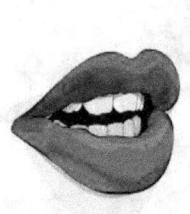  

- *Mouth*
- *Purse*
- *Wild Cat.*

I came to notice also, that (24)

Attracts a Lipstick, (31) most of the time.

A Lady (17) also attracts a Lipstick and Wild Cat or Tiger (05). A Lady again attracts the mouth.

Then again, the Law of Parity...is the ruler of the day.

Numbers and Symbols

- *Ship*
- *Shoes*
- *Car*
- *Bed*
- *Cats*
- *Left Foot*

Another repetition for your advantage, and though some people may be angry with the repetitions, you will soon realize they are actually giving you a greater selection with much Peace of Mind.

Numbers and Symbols

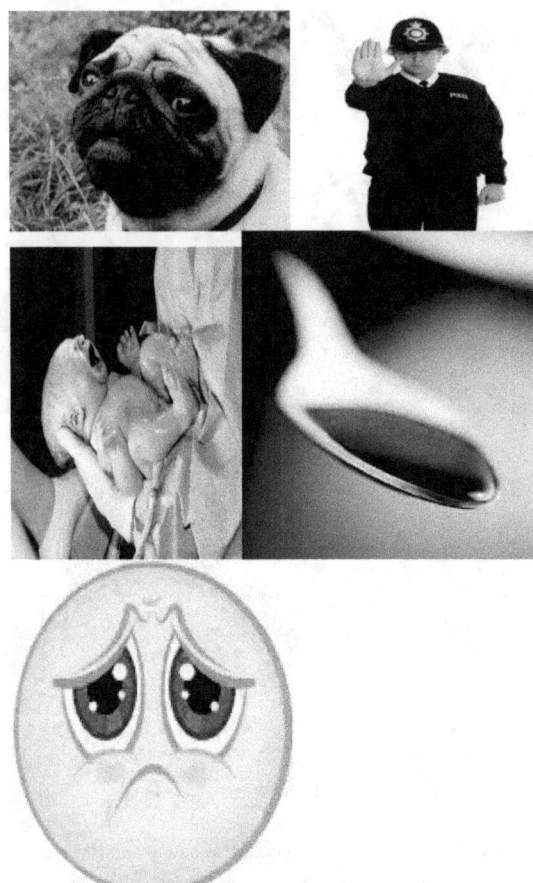

- **Dog**
- **Policeman**
- **Newborn**
- **Medicine**
- **Sad news**

As earlier mentioned, a dog can be any kind, German shepherd, a Chihuahua or any mutt. Medicine can be pills or liquid medicines, can you may be tempted to put up with number 29 as it form part of Small water but not always. By the time you are ready and well educated with the methods, you will be more like a professor and you would know.

Do you also remember that there's a number depicting a child? Can you see the forth bullet point says a newborn?

Consider this dream

...You are in a hospital, sitting next to a Pregnant Woman (8), who is telling you that she wants to have a natural child birth. She wants to deliver through her Vagina (35), but since it's her first, it gives her some Butterflies (18), and she says that, showing her Mouth (24) to you but clenches her Teeth (21). You could almost feel her Excitement (31). And later she comes out showing this baby (27).

Do you see how well you can use the newborn as 27?

Numbers and Symbols

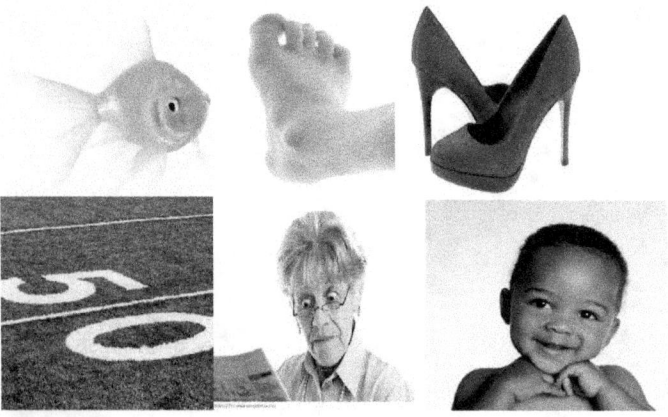

- *Small Fish*
- *Right foot*
- *Shoes*
- *Turf*
- *Surprise*
- *Child*

Here again we cannot over-emphasize the Child issue.

Shoes are shown again giving you that edge of selection.

Small Fish can be a Sardine or a Gold Fish, or Koi or any fish that fits in a bowl or home aquarium.

Numbers and Symbols

- *Chicken (Live one)*
- *Priest*
- *Sun*
- *Forest*
- *Throat*
- *Indian*

As an Indian, the same rule will apply to you as far as your dream is concerned, you can't place

30 as Indian, but can place number 2 as Blackman, number 1 as a Whiteman, number 8 as a Chinese and 17 as white woman. So we have Four Major South African Races represented here. Nice…To conclude on this long chapter, please don't try to memorize these symbols, rather refer back to them in a form of a chart and only visit them when you are placing or mapping your dream. It's the Parity System we can advice to memorize because you can place the numbers anywhere you are by just thinking of the numbers and not the dreams, if you can't get hold of your dram note pad.

The Parity System saves you money and increases your chance of getting back your money and/or wins you a Jackpot. I sometimes use only R10.50 on Power-Ball that I can reuse for almost three months without putting any more money until I bust the numbers of use it unintentionally.

Let's look at this dream:

62 Washington - Lotto	5 Nov 2011	2,15,22,30,31,48 Payout

Dream:

You have this nightmare about this woman with a glossy Lipstick (31), who your husband spend Money (2) and buy her Shoes (22). You later run into her and you call her a Slut (15) and hold her by the Throat (30). You throw her into a Fire (12).

Wow, this is scary.

Let's take a look at this dream:

40 New York - Sweet Million Lotto	3 Nov 2011	2,5,10,16,27,30 Payout

New Yorkers are Dreamers….

You are in a cab, and you talking to an Indian (30) Driver (2), when a Cop (27), stops a cab for speeding. There is an Argument (5) between the two and then they grab each other by their Clothes (16). You abandon the cab and decide to catch a Train (10).

Realistic isn't it? It's like you had this dream yesterday.

The WHEEL of FORTUNE and Lotteries

Chapter 3

The Wheel of Fortune aims to teach and show what Laws and how Parity methods apply to the Fa-fi System. These Paring Methods can also be applied to the South African National Lottery System. Before we show you how, we need to explain the different systems used by Lotto (as we have explained the Fa-Fi systems before) and the Power-Ball as per the South African National Lottery Board (in a nutshell).

1. Fa-Fi Systems and Methods.

This is a 1/36 system.

You select 1 number out of a group of 36.

2. Power-Ball Systems and Methods

This is a 5/45 and 1/20 system.

You need to select 5 numbers out of a group of 45 numbers.

To win the Jackpot, there is a second group of numbers of 20.

The 5 numbers must match the drawn numbers and the Power-Ball must also match the Drawn Power-Ball.

3. Lotto Systems and Methods

This is a 6/49 system.

In order to win a Jackpot, you will need to select 6 numbers out of 49 numbers.

The WHEEL OF FORTUNE will show you that all these Lotteries are reduced to the Fa-Fi Systems and Methods, thus giving you the greater chance of maximizing your chances of winning and taking your Dreams as a guideline.

Let's take a Look, shall we?

The Wheel of Fortune

Remember we told you about a UNIVERSAL *LAW OF PLANETS?*

This is where you get to see the law in action.

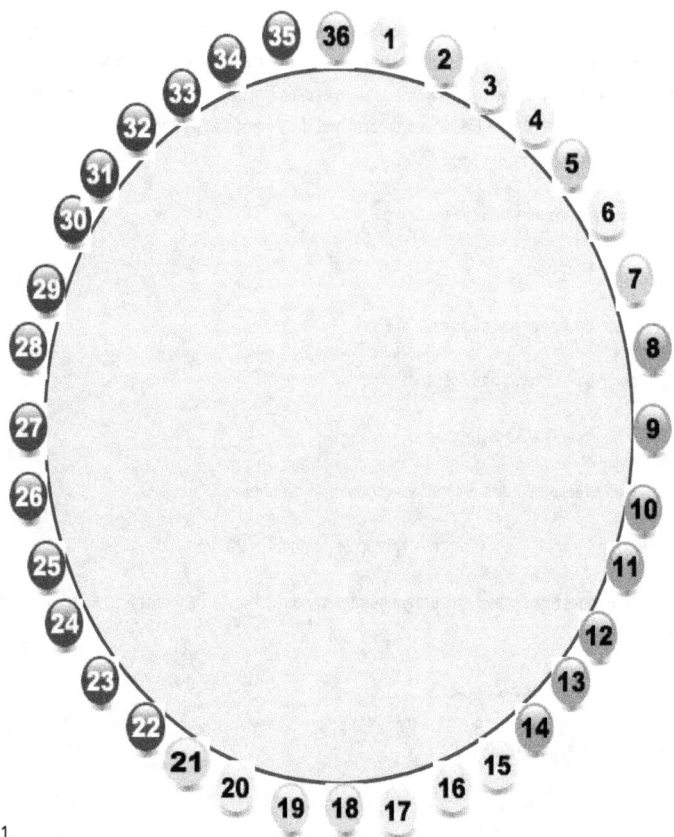

Fig 1

This is a perfect Circle representing the Planetary Movements as far as Fa-Fi is concerned

This is also used to map and plot the Drawn Numbers by day by number. You remove the numbers that are drawn everyday to see your chances of remaining legible numbers.

Looking at the Wheel,

Let's say for an example the numbers 14, 34 and 18 are drawn on Monday, the Wheel of Fortune will look like this by the end of Monday or Tuesday Morning before the Draw.

Fig 2

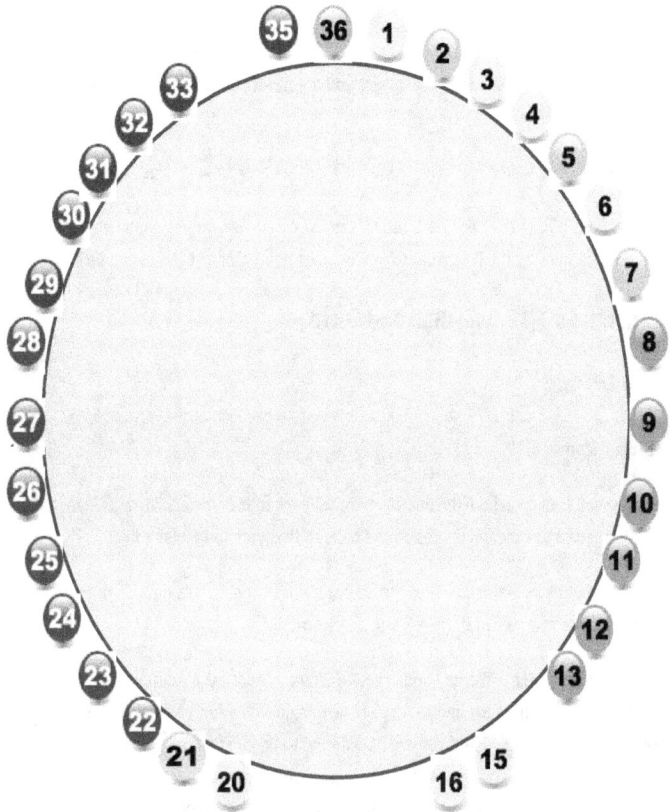

Please note that the Parity Law has selected 14 and 34.

Universal Law of Fa-Fi

Then he selected the closing number 18 in the afternoon. Now, the logic number that the

M'China can possibly open with the next day is **31** (which pairs with 18 in the Parity Law). Even if he doesn't choose to draw the number 31, he needs to obey the Laws and choose numbers compatible to the Law of Parity 14 and 34 and also Parity 18 and 31. These numbers should NOT be in interference of the Movement of 18 and 31 Parity and also The 14 and 34

Parity.

Confused? Don't worry, we are just making sure you are paying attention as it will be clear by the time you end this chapter.

That way, the gamblers would speculate using the methods and dreams to get to the number.

The Wheel of Fortune again, as per Fig 1 above, shows you all 36 numbers neatly placed around the revolution. Remember the 0 degrees to 360 degrees point made? Please keep up with me.

Comparison: Fa-Fi, Power-Ball and Lotto.

- Fa-Fi 1/36 system and
- Power-Ball 5/45 and 1/20 (in a nutshell, this system can also take a form of 6/45).
- Lotto system is 6/49.

The next page will show you how the numbers are set back to the Universal Law of Planetary systems. We need to use the full figures on the page so that you don't miss a thing.

We show you how the numbers assumes the new systems of the Planets outside the universe that we are known to be studying where Fa-fi is concerned.

We also show the Parity Law in detail and in action. You can revisit the example above so that when you come back to the next figures, you are keeping up. We don't want to intellectualize the whole thing like you would as if you are now bound to become a Rocket Scientist. We explained when we started this book that we will use simple easy to understand and easy to use methods. The next figures are very important to your understanding.

Look closely now.

Power-Ball's Wheel of Fortune

Fig 3

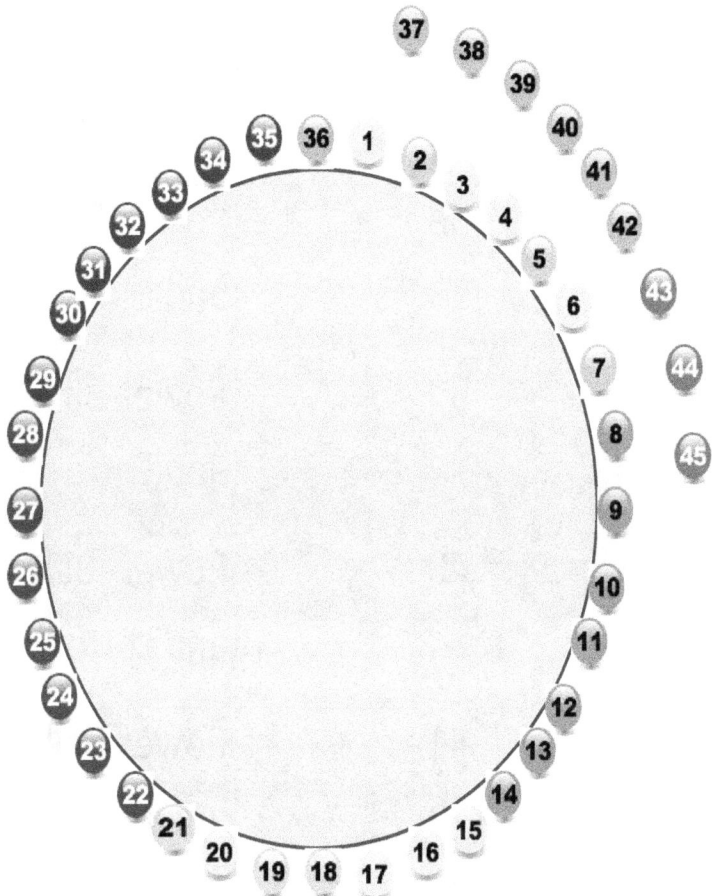

All the Power-Ball system is doing, is assume the new moons or new Planets outside the Universe.

Rather, you say it's the Replica of the existing Planets. The Number 1 is also Number 37.

Table of Extensions

1	37	Power-Ball and Lotto
2	38	Power-Ball and Lotto
3	39	Power-Ball and Lotto
4	40	Power- Ball and Lotto
5	41	Power-Ball and Lotto
6	42	Power-Ball and Lotto
7	43	Power-Ball and Lotto

8	44	Power-Ball and Lotto
9	45	Power-Ball and Lotto
10	46	Lotto
11	47	Lotto
12	48	Lotto
13	49	Lotto

Fig 4

Note: The Table can go on and on until the cycle repeat itself. Your Country may use a system of 6/72.

Don't dismay, all you need to do is to go with the cycle until you get to 72. The dreams are all restricted to 36, which mean if you dream of a King, you will either choose 1 or 37.

Points to Ponder

- Dreams Symbols don't change
- Parity Laws don't change
- Law of 36 doesn't change (we will deal with this later)
- *Some countries go up to 80 Number System but the numbers still revolve around the Initial Universal Law of 360 degrees or 36 Number System.*
- To nip it in a butt, and our emphasis, please look at fig 5 below

Fig 5

The Parity System Explained

Chapter 4

Parity Laws says: **In a Perfect Universe, Numbers Will Respect the Movements of Their Counterparts and will NOT Interfere with them in their Own Orbits.**

We are taking South African National Lotteries Power-Ball and Lotto as Example

| Partner A | Partner B | Associate A | Associate B |

1	36	37	
2	29	38	
3	8	39	44
4	15	40	
4	35	40	
5	19	41	
6	33	42	
7	13	43	49
9	17	45	
10	23	46	
11	26	47	
12	34	48	
14	32	Etc	
16	35	Etc	
18	31	Etc	
20	25	Etc	
21	24	Etc	
22	27	Etc	
26	30	Etc	
28	30	Etc	

Looking at the table above, now you can see how the Parity Law operates. You will be much clearer when we are done showing the Parity Law using the Wheel of Fortune.

Let's go back a little and show a dream example from the previous real life Lotto Results.

This is the Philippines Lotto Results as at 9 November 2011

The Dream:

You see yourself living large with a Mansion (25) and you are out fishing (21). Your increases and you get this Big Fish (49 also 13). You get into your Car (47 also 11) and drive home and on the driveway, you get a warm welcome form you Little Girl (19) who takes you in the house. Your first sight is this warm glowing Fire (12) in the grand hall. You thank the lord for your blessings and suddenly...you wake up. You have been dreaming:

Note:

- 25 is Big House
- 21 is a Fisherman
- 13 is Big Fish
- 11 is a Car
- 19 is Young Girl
- 12 is Fire

Also Note:

- 13 is also 49 which this Draw has 49 selected.
- 11 is also 47 which this Draw has 47 selected.
- *Parity 21 and 24 has been selected.(page 71 shows Parity Law of 21 and 24)*

The Parity Law 2 and 29

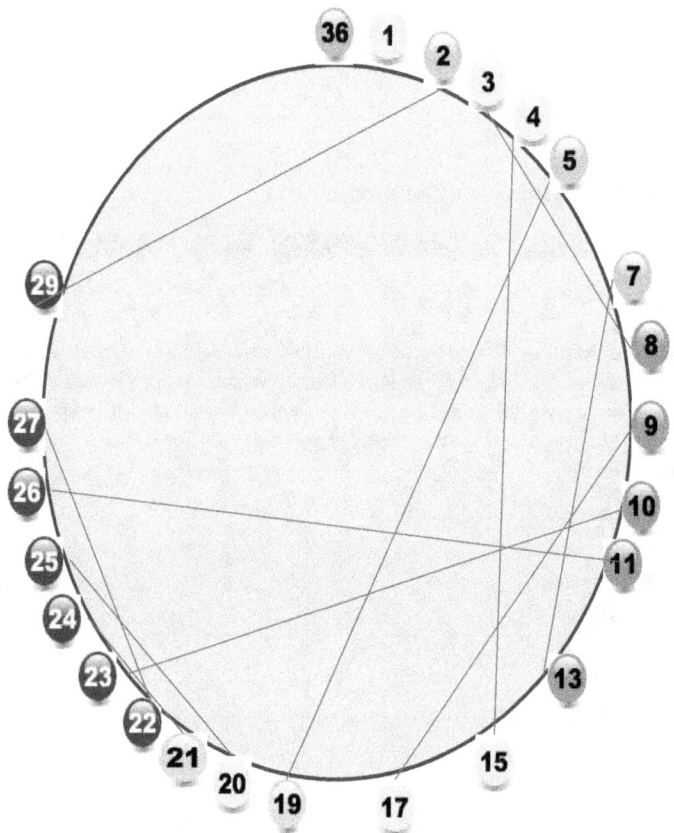

The Numbers restricted to share the spotlight are:

6, 33,

12, 32,

14, 34,

16, 35,

18, 31,

28, 30 and note that there is no line crossing a 2 and 29 *connecting line*

The Parity Law 3 and 8

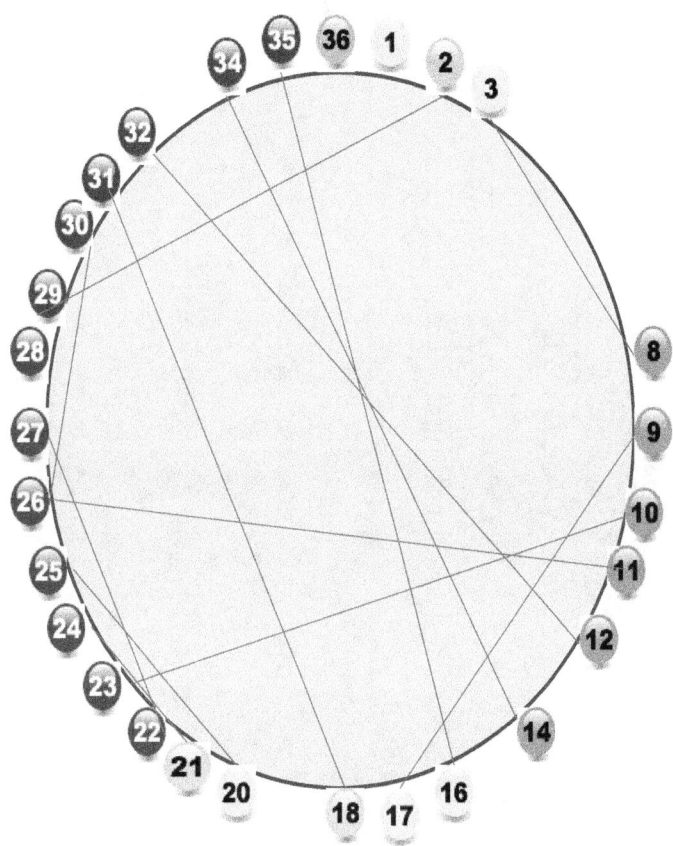

Restrictions are to:

4, 15
5, 19
6, 33
7, 13

And note that there is no line that crosses the 3 and 8 *connecting line*

The Parity Law 4 and 15

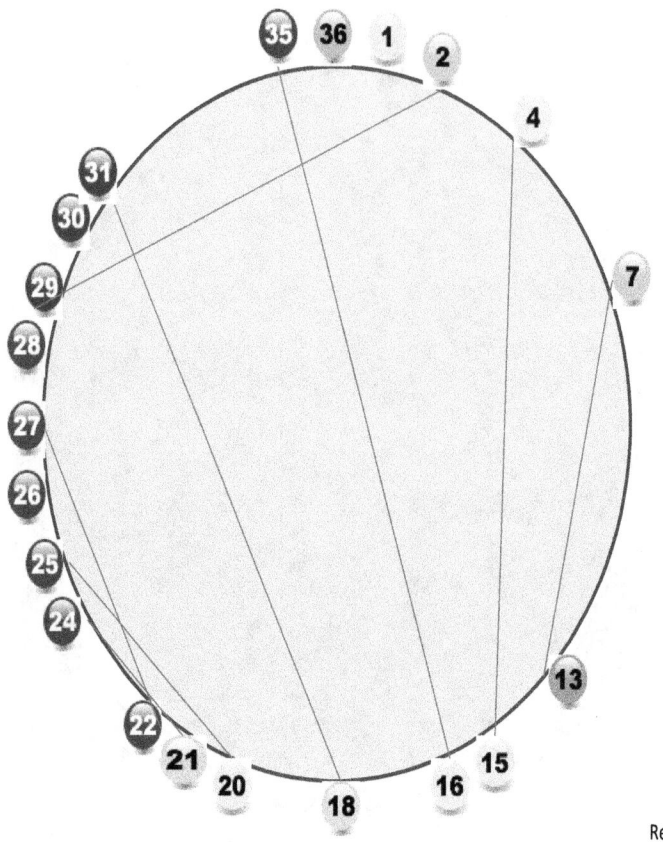

Restricti

ons:

3, 8

5, 19

6, 33

9, 17

10, 23

11

12, 32 and 14, 34 and note there's no line that crosses the 4 and 15 *connecting line*

The Parity Law 4 and 35

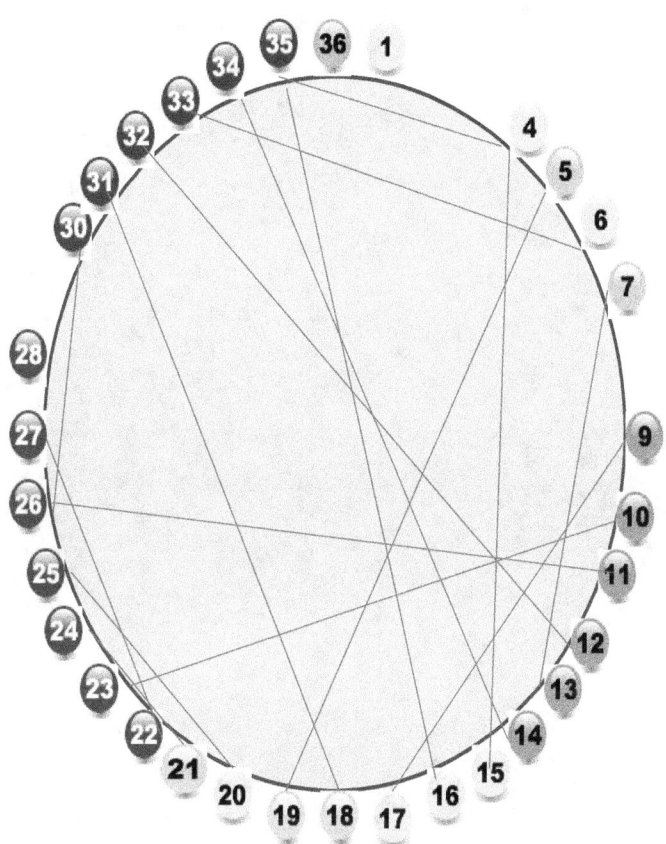

Restrictions:
3, 8
2, 29

And note there's no line that crosses the 4 and 35 *connecting line*

The Parity Law 5 and 19

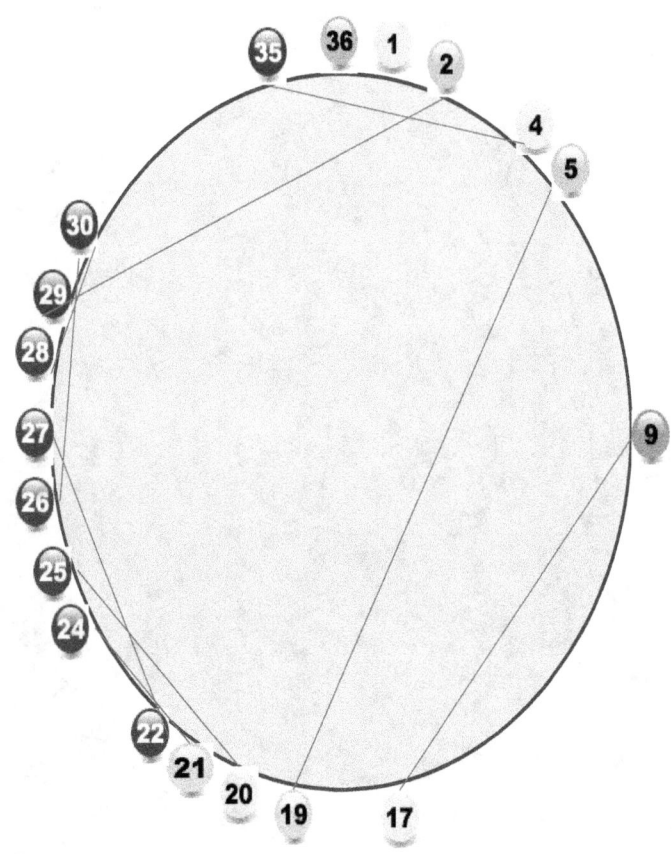

Restrictions:

3, 8

6, 33

7, 13

10, 23

11, 15, 12, 32,

14, 34, 18, 31 and note: no line that crosses 5 and 19 *connecting line*

The Parity Law 6 and 33

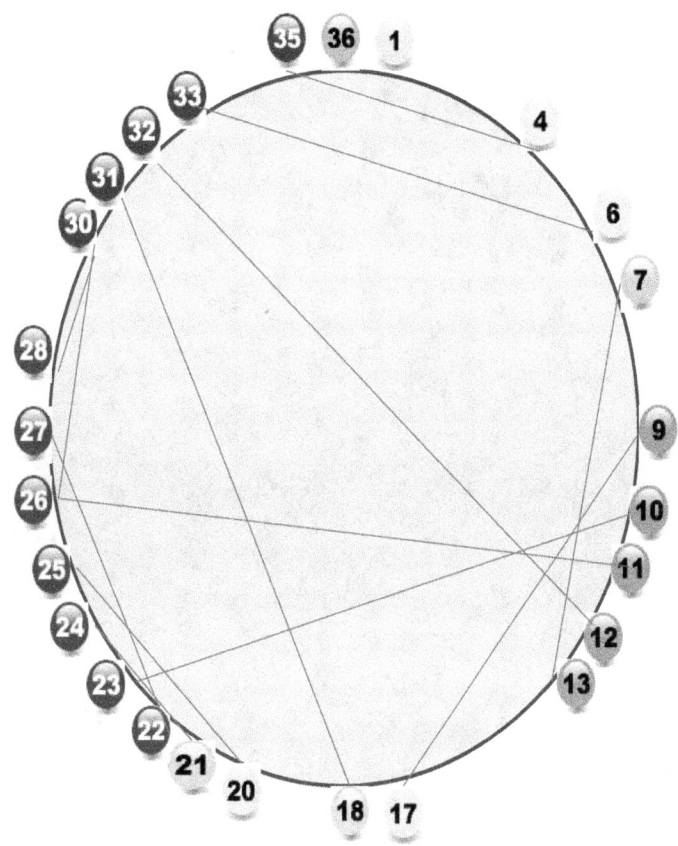

Restrictions:

2, 29

3, 8

5, 19

14, 34

15

16 and note that there's no line that crosses the 6 and 33 *connecting line*

The Parity Law 7 and 13

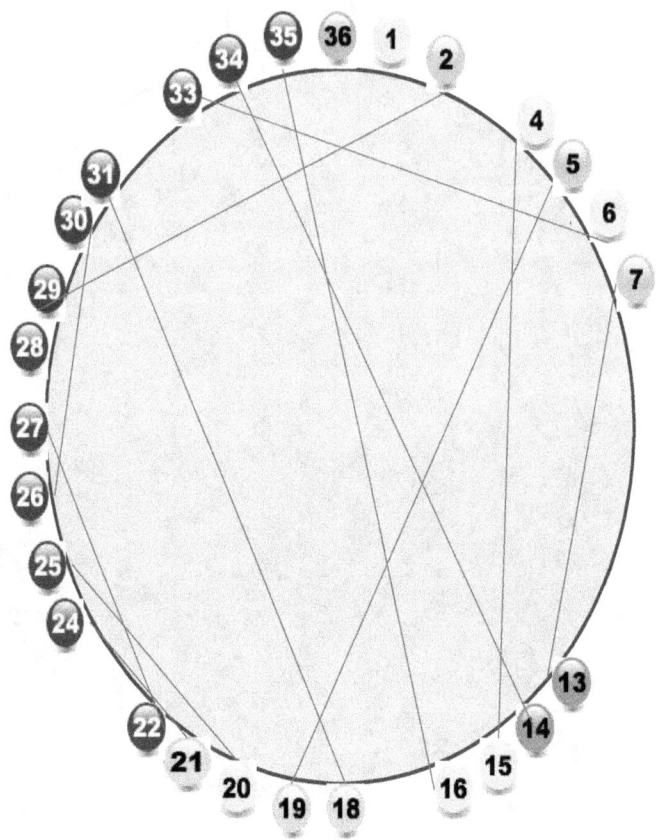

Restrictions:

3, 8

9, 17

10, 23

11

12, 32

And note that there's no line that crosses the 7 and 13 *connecting line*

The Parity Law 9 and 17

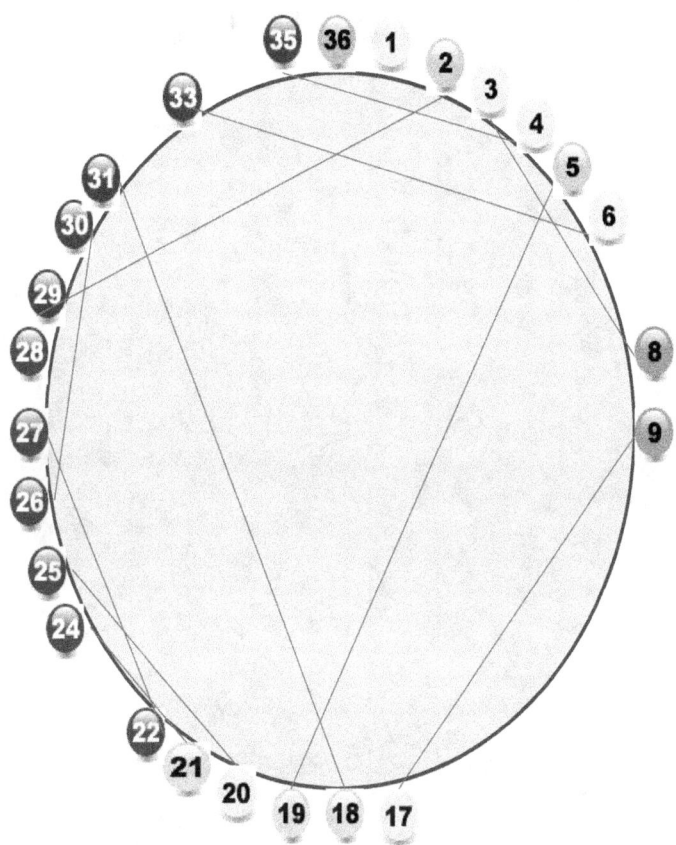

Restrictions:

7, 13

10, 23

11

12, 32

14, 34

15, 16, and note that there's no line that crosses the 9 and 17 *connecting line*

The Parity Law 10 and 23

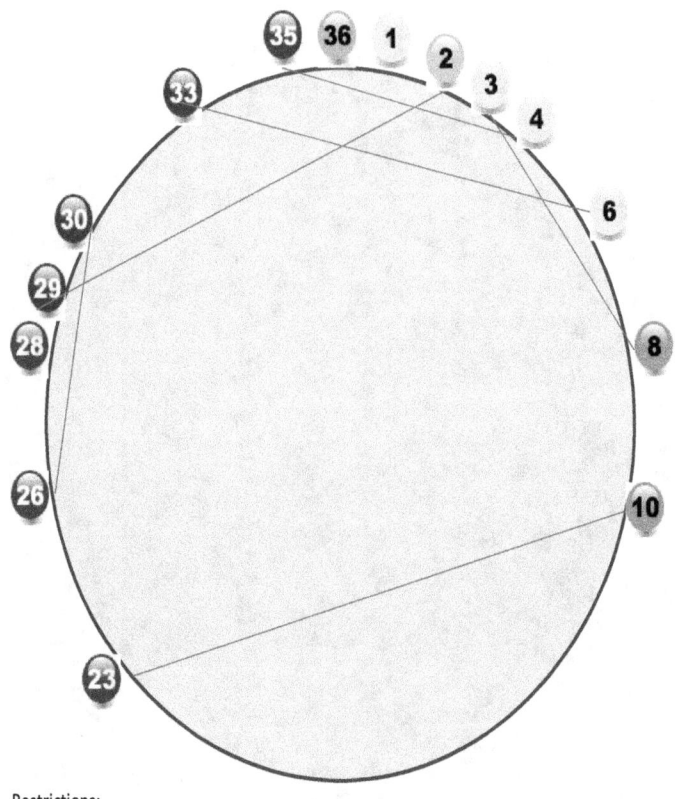

Restrictions:

5, 19

7, 13

9, 17

11, 26

12, 32

14, 34

16,

18, 31,

20, 25, 21, 24, 22, 27 and note there's no line that crosses the 10 and 23 *connecting line*

The Parity Law 11 and 26

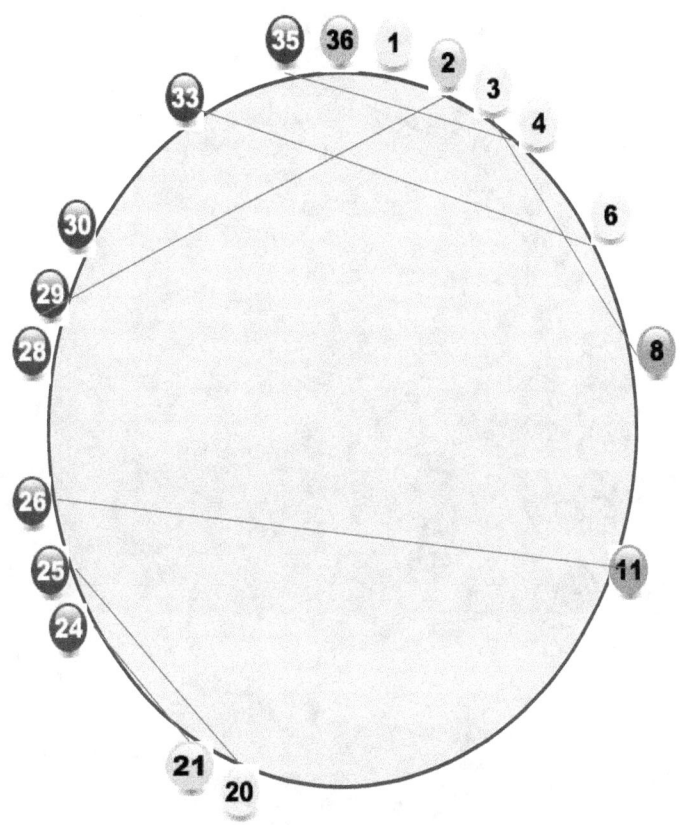

Restrictions:

5, 19
7, 13
9, 17
10, 23
12, 32,
14, 34, 16,
18, 31,
22, 27 and note that there's no line that crosses the 11 and 26 *connecting line*

The Parity Law 12 and 32

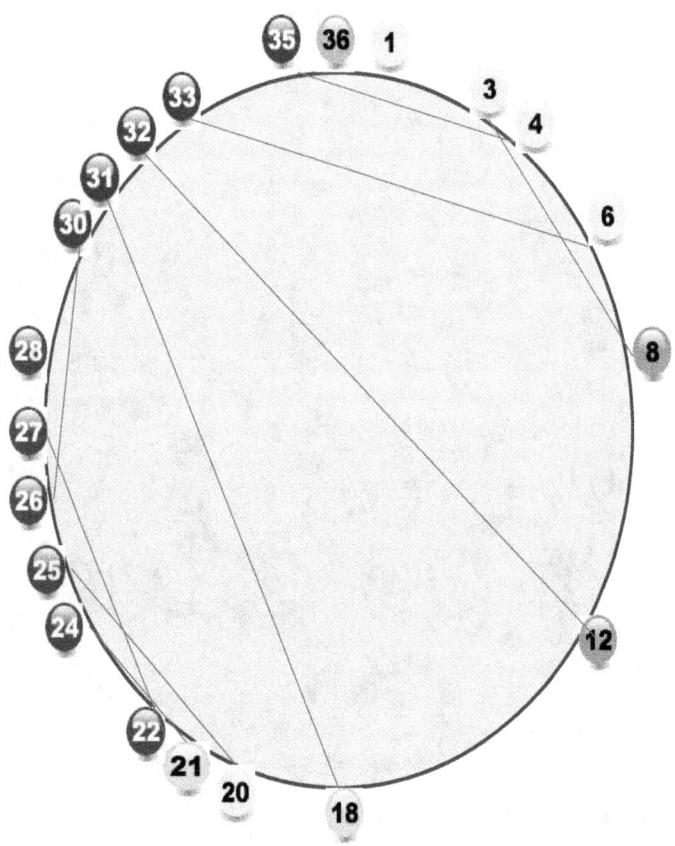

Restrictions:

2, 29

5, 19

7, 13

9, 17

10, 23

11, 14, 34, 16, and note that there's no line that crosses the 12 and 32 *connecting line*

The Parity Law 14 and 34

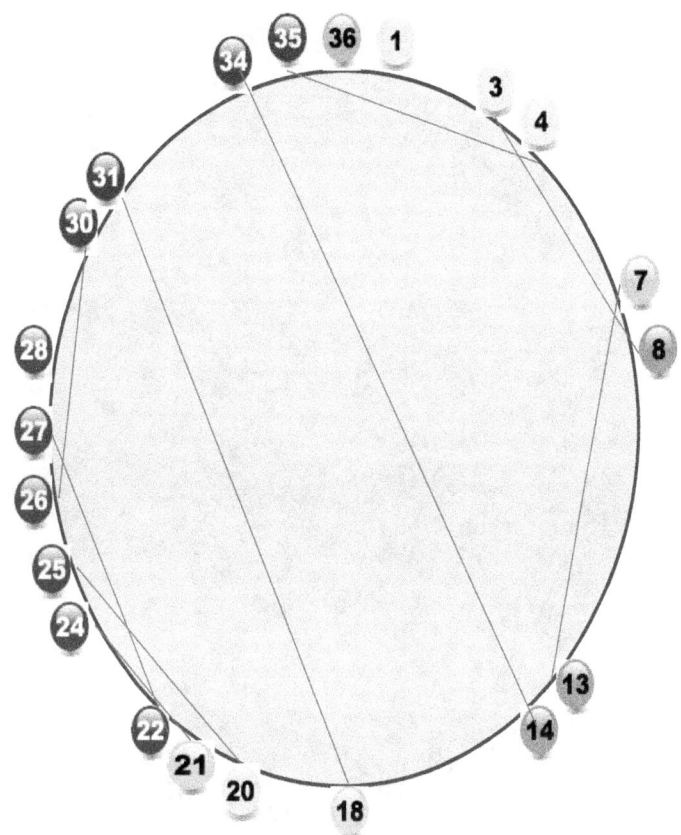

Restrictions:

2, 29

5, 19

6, 33

9, 17

10, 23

11

12, 32, 15, 16, and note that there's no line that crosses the 14 and 34 *connecting line*

The Parity Law 16 and 35

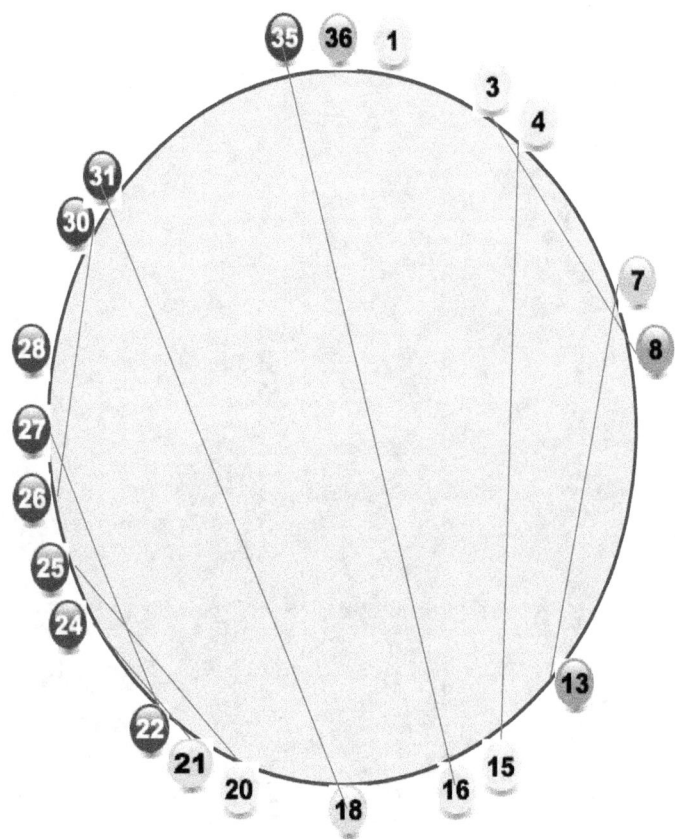

Restrictions:

5, 19
6, 33
9, 17
10, 23
11
12, 32
14, 34, and note that there's no line that crosses the 16 and 35 *connecting line*

The Parity Law 18 and 31

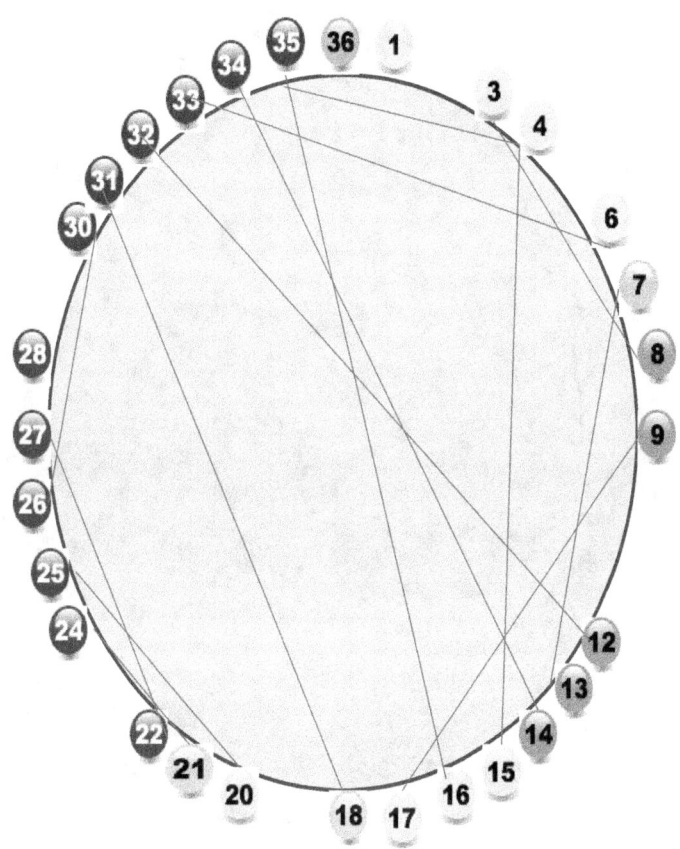

Restrictions:
2, 29
5, 19
10, 23
11

And note that there's no line that crosses the 18 and 31 *connecting line*

The Parity Law 20 and 25 & 21 and 24

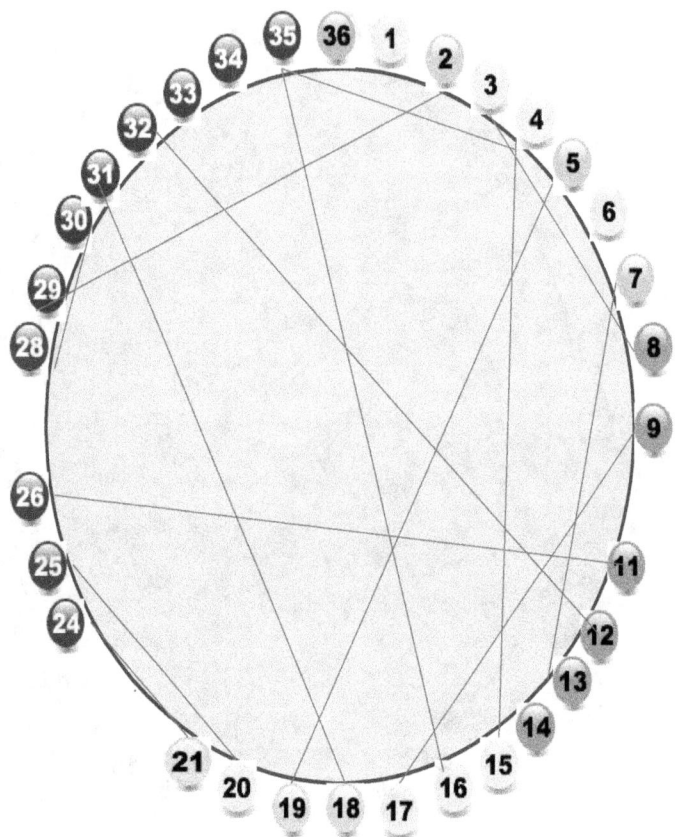

Restrictions;
22, 27

And note that there's no line that crosses the 20 and 25, 21 and 24 *connecting line*

The Parity Law 22 and 27

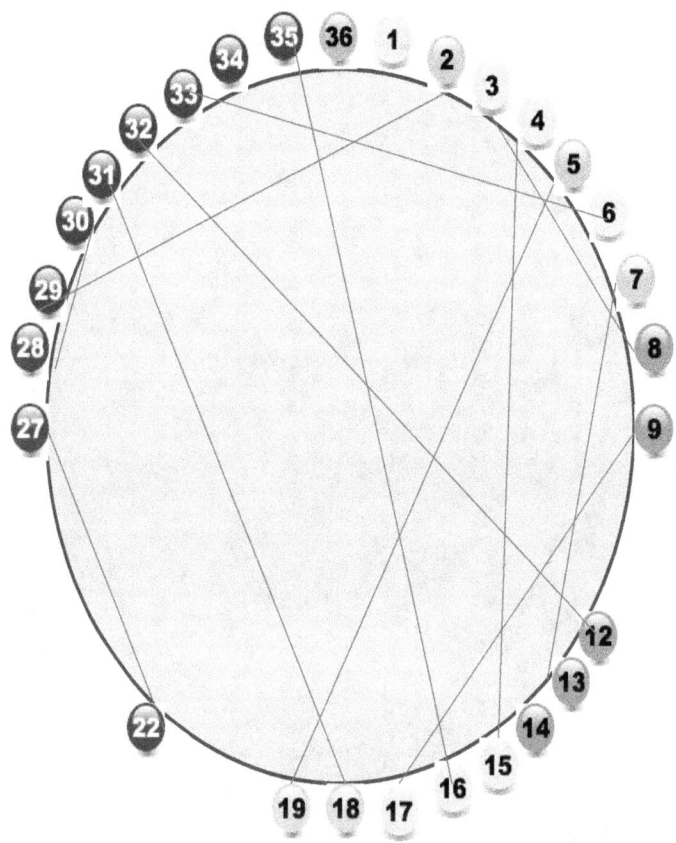

Restrictions:

10, 23
11, 26
20, 25
21, 24

And note that there's no line that crosses the 22 and 27 *connecting line*

The Parity Law 26, 28 and 30

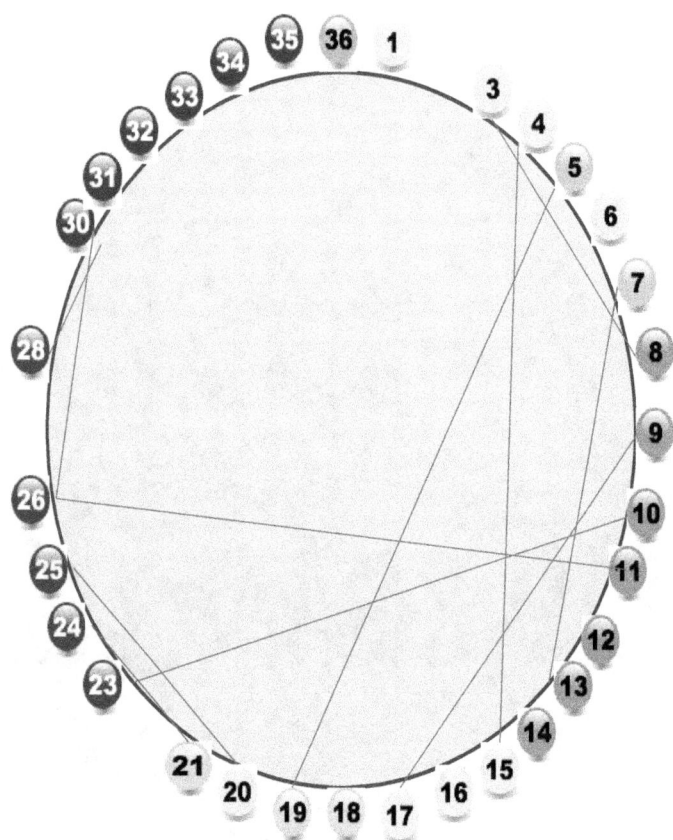

Restrictions:
2, 29
22, 27

And note that there's no line that crosses the 26 and 30, also 28 and 30 *connecting line*

In Conclusion

Using the Number Chart with Latest Results, remove all the numbers that have been selected, and you will only be left with numbers limited enough to give you an advantageous edge

Draw Date	Ball 1	Ball 2	Ball 3	Ball 4	Ball 5	Power-Ball
11/8/2011	8	10	11	15	45	
11/4/2011	34	31	9	25	42	
11/1/2011	34	23	43	39	13	
10/28/2011	3	41	37	15	36	
10/25/2011	38	12	20	11	35	
10/21/2011	42	2	39	16	23	
10/18/2011	2	32	12	8	15	
10/14/2011	20	15	21	35	31	
10/11/2011	24	39	8	43	10	
10/7/2011	38	36	33	40	44	
10/4/2011	26	40	42	10	8	
9/30/2011	28	24	35	11	21	

This is the Numbers Drawn Chart.

- Create a Wheel Of Fortune
- Remove the numbers that have already been drawn previously
- Work around the Hot and numbers and the remaining numbers
- Check your Dreams and refer to the Number Chart for selection. (this will be explained in details using all the notes used here)

Remaining Numbers

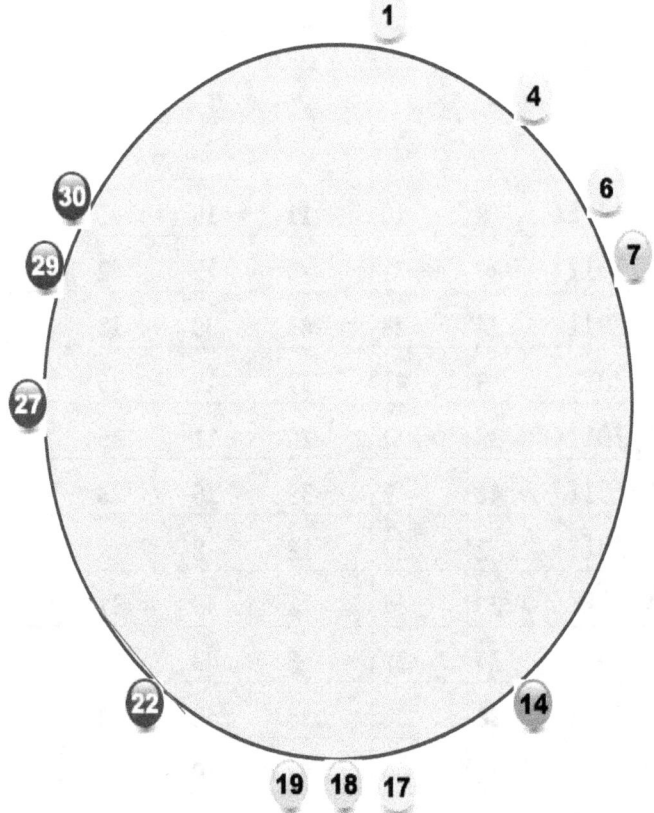

After you have removed all the selected numbers from previous draws, you have a much clearer picture of what and where you should be concentrating.

The Challenge would be the combination of the new and the old Hot and Cold Numbers. This when you rely on your gut feel to help you choose the right number combination.

Parity Law of 22 and 27 stands here. And the restricted numbers are not there.

The Law of

Chapter 4

The Law of 36 explains that...*With every draw of 6 numbers and more, two or more numbers have to add to 35/36.*

This rule is adhered to by many movements of the numbers drawn, with few anomalies. Like any other system, the Law of 36 has some undesired deviations that throw the ball game out of Balance.

When playing Fa-Fi, M'China sticks to the Laws of the Game and the Parity System as truly and honestly as possible. Somehow, the Boss would be prone to make mistakes and throw the game out of balance.

A series of events would take place. Namely:

- A Number would be selected and it will throw the game out of bounce.

When this happens, most people lose their bets to the M'China's advantage. This normally doesn't last for him as this would catch up with him later, in a few days time.

- Because of the Anomaly, somehow the numbers are sent into a frenzy of some sort, making the selection to be more predictable.

When this happens, the M'China would be in a situation so bizarre that more than half of his stations would be able to predict the winning numbers so much that he would run out of money to pay for the bets.

THIS IS A PROCESS WHEN HE DECLARES THE "BAG TO BE BURNT"

The law of Parity and his Law of 36, governing his Game's Universe, would be compromised so much that he would need to start the "RUN" afresh.

Don't you ever wish the Lotto Bodies or Companies were to explain why out of 14 million bets, there is not even a single ticket winning the jackpot but they are sitting with 100 000 tickets with 3 numbers and a bonus ball?

Law of 36 as drawn from Previous Draws

Let's look at this Law in Action

Pick six dreams. This reminds me of my late granny. She loved to bet on the horse called Spanish Pool.

Let's see what her dream could have been...or yours.

You park your Car (11), and get to the subway to take a Train (46 also 10) to work. To your Surprise (28), a Gentleman (42 also 6) approaches you and ask for a 10 Dollars (38 also 2), you tell him that he is asking for a Fortune (4) but you give him anyway.

A Good Samaritan dream...maybe the person you gave money to in your dream, could have been...y'know...the messenger of God.

Law of 36

4	11	28	38	42	46

38, 28 and 42 gives you 36.

38 is (2), and 42 is (6)

Also remember that when you do you selection, you take numbers in their natural (1 to 36) then according to your Country's Lotto System, you can convert them to your desired numbers

Dream:

" ...you know of a Teary (29) Funeral (26), of a Old Woman (14) who has left her King son (1 also 37) and her Queen (17) daughter in law a Fortune (4).

Law Of 36

1	4	14	17	26	29	37

A perfect straight line 36.

More???

Okay, let's indulge you a little.

11 Canada - Lotto 649   5 Nov 2011   14,18,22,34,36,43 3 Payout

Dream:

"...you see an Old Woman (14), in the Rain (18) going through the Dirt (34), holding a Cigar (36) in one hand a Big Stick (43 also 7). Frogs (3) jumping next to the old woman's bare feet as she saved her Shoes (22)."

Just another Day in paradise hey...

Law Of 36

14	18	22	34	36	43	3

14, 18 and 3 = 35

8 Brazil - Mega-Sena   5 Nov 2011   1,6,8,10,25,27 Payout

The Land of Great People, here is your conversion.

"You dream of your cousin who is a wanted by Cops (27) because he robbed a Mansion (25). You are so furious that you call him a Cow (6). However, you take him to a Train (10) station. You leave to buy some ticket only to come back to find him Drunk (8) and Bloody (1)

Law of 36

1	6	8	10	25	27

1 …8…27…=36

7 ▮▮ Belgium - Lotto   5 Nov 2011   4,14,21,25,33,42 39 Payout

Your DREAM:

"Your Mother (14) is telling you of your Late Father's (4) secrets of fathering some Boys (33). You tell her that your father was such a Gentleman (42 also 6) and he worked hard to provide her with a Big House (25). She also tell you that your father died of a stab wound {a Knife} (21) and not by an Accident (39 also 3) and you cry frantically"

Scary!!!

Law of 36

4	14	21	25	33	42	39

14 and 21=35   please look for some combinations here.

6 ▭ Austria - Lotto   2 Nov 2011   4,23,31,32,36,45 28 Payout

Austrian Dreamer:

"Your Doctor (23) charges you a Fortune (4) for your Child (45 also 9) health, and you decide to take it up with him. You then take it to the Bishop (31) but you are Surprised (28) as he asks you for more Paper

Money (32). You tell him that he is such a Dick (36) and you walk out."

Law Of 36

4	23	31	32	36	45	28

4 and 32 is 36   31 and 4 is 35   23 and 9 and 4 is 36

4 🗺 Australia - Saturday Lotto   5 Nov 2011   2,6,12,18,44,45 28,32 Payout

My...my...my!

"You consoling a Gentleman (6) who just found out that his Pregnant (44 also 8) wife is Dead (12), while giving birth to their Baby (45 also 9). You get Surprised (28) as he mentions the Money (2) he is going to get and that he says he is going to blow on Gold (32) stock. He will only give his mother in law some Small change (18)"

Law of 36

2	6	12	18	44	45	28	32	

2...6...18 and 45 gives you 35.

3 🗺 Australia - Powerball Lotto   3 Nov 2011   2,5,18,22,44 9 Payout

Let's check the Power-Ball. Here's your Dream...

"You are Drunk (8) and looking for a lift in the Rain (18), you try to run but lose your Shoe (22). You finally decide to take a cab but you have no Money (2). Then you meet up with a Muscular Guy (5) and you walk with him home under the Moonlight (9)"

It's a complicated dream like any other but the dream nonetheless.

Law of 36

2	5	18	22	44	9

35 is what you get right?

2 Australia - Oz Lotto   1 Nov 2011   5,12,17,23,25,31,44 13,19 Payout

Wow, this must a headache to choose number from. The mind, although complex, cannot remember so many numbers from a dream. The most numbers a mind can remember is only three numbers.

Dream:

"A Queen (12) Lady (17) taking her pet Tiger (5) for a walk around the Castle (25), and she constantly touches her Crown (23). She reaches for her Lipstick (31) when she sees a Chinese (44 also 8) gardener to entice him. She touches her tigers Tail (13) as she passes by. She sits to take a Smoke (19)."

Law of 36

5	12	17	23	25	31	44	13	19

I will let you do your own 36 calculation here. There is much more to choose from.

63 Wisconsin - Megabucks   5 Nov 2011   2,18,33,45,46,48 Payout

I just love how People from Wisconsin pronounce the word: Wisconsin.

Your Dream:

It's Christmas and you have your Boys (33) asking you for Money (2) to buy some chocolate Eggs (46 also 10). You search for some Coins (18) but you cant find any. You ask them to join you by the Fire (48 also

12) where you have prepared them a lovely Dish (45 also 9)

Nice warm dream for Christmas.

Law of 36

2	18	33	45	46	48

2 + 33 is 35...easy way out huh.

Please find other combinations???

62 Washington - Lotto   5 Nov 2011 2,15,22,30,31,48 Payout

Dream:

You have this nightmare about this woman with a glossy Lipstick (31), who your husband spend Money (2) and buy her Shoes (22). You later run into her and you call her a Slut (15) and hold her by the Throat (30). You throw her into a Fire (12).

The Law of 36

2	15	22	30	31	48

2, 22 and 48 gives you 36.

61 Vermont - Megabucks Plus   5 Nov 2011 9,11,20,21,25 2 Payout

Dream:

You dream of spending Money (2) on this Mansion (25) because you are expecting a Baby (9). You also want to sell your Car (11) and your Music (20) collection. You smile at that thought so much your Teeth (21) are showing.

Remember folks, dreams usually don't make sense. Find the Essence of it and carry on.

Law Of 36

9	11	20	21	25	2

9,25 and 2 = 36.

60	U.S.A. - Powerball	5 Nov 2011	2,33,39,40,43 26 Payout

Here is another one which is interesting.

You are attending a Funeral (26) of A Crooked (43 also 7) Driver Pilot (2) who died (40 also 4) through an Airplane (33) Accident (39 also 3).

Power-Ball and Mega Millions are not having great dreams BUT there's GREAT Money.

Law Of 36

2	33	39	40	43	26

35 is your answer...Perfect!

59	U.S.A. - Mega Millions	4 Nov 2011	26,30,32,33,44 1 Payout

Mega Dreams for Mega Millions...These are big numbers here. I bet the dream is sweet also.

You are attending a Funeral (26) where a Fat (44 also 8) Priest (30) is preaching. Suddenly a very Drunk (8) Ill-mannered wife (32) starts to sob uncontrollably, saying her King (1) is dead. This had some Young Boy (33) giggling.

This dream isn't sweet at all but it could have made you a millionaire.

Law of 36

26	30	32	33	44	1

Aah..35 is what you get when you add the highlighted numbers.

16 Connecticut - Classic Lotto	4 Nov 2011 4,6,7,8,15,17 Payout

The Dream and Numbers:

You see a Gentleman (6) who has quite a fortune (4) who somehow, has married a crooked (7) Lady (17), who sometimes behaves like a whore (15) when drunk (8).

The Dreams are quite simple and so should be the number selection.

Law Of 36

4	6	7	8	15	17

The highlighted numbers add up to 36.

The Numbers that won $245 Million Power-Ball

00 U.S.A. - Powerball	12,14,34,39,46 36 Payout

Law of 36

12	14	34	39	46	+36

Now, go back to the Wheel of Fortune and Look at the number 39...3 right?

Now look back again at number 46...10 right?

The law of 36 says you must have 2 or more numbers adding up to 35...or 36.

12	14	34	3	10	+36

Now add 12, to 14, to 10 and you get a perfect 36.

A person could have had dream where he is in a hospital where a Chinese (12) Nurse (14), bringing him a piece of Steak (34). Instead he finds himself being fondled and his Balls (10) and Penis (36) being massaged. That leads to a vigorous Sex (3).

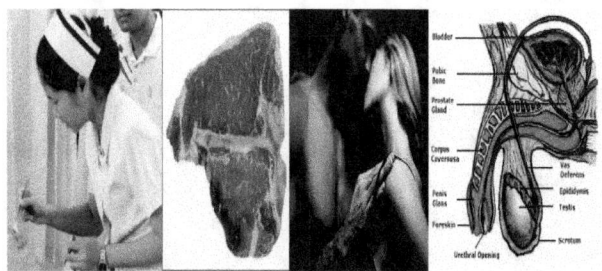

It sounds Silly, but very possible to have this dream. This would have made you $245 Million Wealthy.

The Numbers selected, shows a Parity of The Moon Rule (Parity 1 and 36).

Binary Code System

Chapter 5

The Law of 36 has a great assistant which helps the process of selection run a little smooth.

The Computer Language coding that you can do for yourself using your Microsoft Excel spreadsheet.

Look at this example.

Binary Chart

	Ball 1	Ball 2	Ball 3	Ball 4	Ball 5	Ball 6	*Value to 35/36*
0							*0*

1							0
2							0
3							0
4							0
5							0
6							0
7							0
8							0
9							0
10							0
11							0
12							0
13							0
14							0
15							0
16							0
17							0
18							0
19							0
20							0

The Green Shaded Area represents the Computer Language or Binary Coding.

Binary Code System

Now let's look at the numbers for better understanding.

Binary Chart 2 of South African Power- Ball Results (In their Natural Form)

Ball 1	Ball 2	Ball 3	Ball 4	Ball 5	Ball 6	Value to 36
6	2	3	16	23	9	36
2	32	12	8	15	13	35
20	15	21	35	31	5	35
24	3	8	7	10	8	35
2	36	33	4	8	4	35
26	4	6	10	8	4	36
28	24	35	11	21	17	35

22	4	1	8	7	18	35
24	27	25	22	5	5	35
8	23	31	10	2	8	35
3	2	28	2	4	20	35
5	11	8	17	28	20	36
4	36	10	23	18	4	36
30	1	5	4	2	3	36
15	9	34	7	25	1	35
2	19	4	5	1	15	36
10	3	20	36	18	13	36
20	4	31	17	22	13	35
28	5	19	21	14	11	35
21	3	16	10	22	9	35
8	5	2	3	7	16	36

Now I am very sure that you are clearer.

Tip: Try not to intellectualize the whole process to a Rocket Scientist Level. Keep it Short and Simple.

The Idea is to Start Interpret your Dream or Selection in a simple way and then you get technical using the Conversion System, The Parity System, The Wheel of Fortune, The Binary System and then you do your Final Selection.

Formation: Binary Coding

Now explore the language in the Computer sense. You do remember that the Computer language uses zeros and one's right?

For every green shaded block, that is your 1 and for every clear block, that is your 0. Let's have more fun.

Binary Chart 3 showing the Computer language

Formation	Ball 1	Ball 2	Ball 3	Ball 4	Ball 5	Ball 6	Value to 36
111101	6	2	3	16	23	9	36
101101	2	32	12	8	15	13	35

110000	20	15	21	35	31	5	35
111000	24	3	8	7	10	8	35
101000	2	36	33	4	8	4	35
101001	26	4	6	10	8	4	36
010100	28	24	35	11	21	17	35
111100	22	4	1	8	7	18	35
001111	24	27	25	22	5	5	35
010110	8	23	31	10	2	8	35
111100	3	2	28	2	4	20	35
011100	5	11	8	17	28	20	36
101011	4	36	10	23	18	4	36
111000	30	1	5	4	2	3	36
010011	15	9	34	7	25	1	35
110001	2	19	4	5	1	15	36
011001	10	3	20	36	18	13	36
000011	20	4	31	17	22	13	35
011001	28	5	19	21	14	11	35
001101	21	3	16	10	22	9	35
101111	8	5	2	3	7	16	36

Closure

Let's recap the process by mapping it in a schematic presentation.

We hope your Dreams Help You Win the Fortune as your heart desires.

Online Resources

You are welcome to visit our blog site for more fun and weekly Dreams Interpretation using this fun Fa-Fi system.

We have posted a number of posts, using the results of the most recent International using most of major sites around the world.

We also publish the site Stats, showing the growth and support of all the viewers as they visit our site.

We also have a Facebook page where people do inbox us a lot for personal dream interpretations sessions.

Visit: http://mydreamismykey.blogspot.com

Join us on Facebook: My Dream Is My Key

We also do partake in most of the affiliated site where Dreams are discussed.

History of the Author

Short History

Royal History of The Mampeule Family

The rich history of Dreams begins way back in the late 1600's, in a historical village known as Khethlakhone, where a mighty and powerful King of the Balovhedu Tribe ruled part of the now known as Limpopo Province, South Africa. The King had a Queen whose dreams were so powerful, that they were unmistakably turned true. It is mentioned that although the Queen had these Dreams powers, the King did not pay attention and even take heed to them.

During that era, most tribes were fighting to increase their rule and would attacked and conquer other villages nearby and far. It was a common thing to find warriors leaving their homes and families to go and join the war in greater distances. Like any war being a one big drag, most wives were left without husbands and children, fatherless. The Balovhedu tribe was not that powerful as the Zulu tribes.

One day, the great King sought to increase his kingdom by going to farther places down south of Africa. He prepared his troops for a great departure.

That night, the Queen had a dream of a great battle loss, and she woke up to tell the husband. Stubborn as he was, he chose to ignore the warning of the Queen's dream. He woke up and prepared his troops and went straight to war. All people cheered for the troops and wished them a bon voyage, as they were confident of their great Ruler. The Queen sat there being sad that she is not going to see her husband again.

Days passed without any word from the troops. Then weeks and then months and then years. Later on, the villages accepted that a great defeat has been experienced.

The great Queen carried on with her duties to rule the tribe and everyone accepted her as the Ruler of the Day. Men and women alike would carry orders from the Queen through the Royal council and life went on normally, with the villagers taking heed on the warning and signs of either success or failures of the years and years to come.

Then a traveler from the North came to the village, tired and hurt. He was taken to the Queen for questioning as it would be a norm for in any village. Then traveler introduced himself and explained his story of him being a powerful advisor to the king of the North, now known as Zimbabwe, who was now afraid of his popularity growing to phenomenon heights, that the villagers were now consulting him for advice rather than listening to the King. He fled the north due to the fact that the king wanted to kill him.

The Queen's mercy was shown to the stranger, and he was shown to a guest house. Later he was given his own land and he and his family were treated with great respect and was cared for. The Queen, having noted his ability to interpret some of her Dreams, decided to make him part of the Royal advisors. As the story unfolds, the stranger claimed to have powers of controlling the weather, or to put it simple, he told the Queen of his innate abilities to make it rain. He was put to a test, and the legend goes, he passed it with flying colors. Now the stranger's popularity grew to greater heights.

As history unfolded, the great Queen was nearing her grave, and it is told that she asked the rain maker, to take the Queen's daughter for a wife, so that he can rule the tribe when she dies. And it came to pass when the great Queen died; the rain maker became the new King of the Balovhedu tribe. It is said that he brought great rains in the region and the neighboring kingdoms heard of this, and started paying a great respect towards the Balovhedu people.

Later in life, the new King saw something in his sons that he didn't appreciate. Then he decided that, in order to preserve the kingdom, so that the greedy sons should not rule the tribe, it is said that he decided to pass his powers to her daughter. It was quite obvious back then that he or she who had the key to the rain making secrets, is the Ruler Of The Day. When the king died, the daughter became the Ruler of the Balovhedu tribe. She was equally respected by the nations of Africa who knew and brought her gifts. Her kingdom was never attacked even by the mighty King of the Zulus himself.

Now that a new Queen was ruling, an agreement between the First Queen and the later Rain maker had to stand. The Queen, although a woman, had to choose a "wife" from the First Queen's family. A daughter from the Chief advisor's family had to be given to the Queen, as a first wife. This was the only way it kept the Royal Blue Blood Preservation going and the Honor of the Royal Agreement. Since then it was passed from Queen to the princess for centuries to pass. The agreement never included the males, but a son from the initial king, would be the Chief Advisor to the Royal Council and the Queen. This also had every chief advisor, to hand his daughter to the Queen a wife.

The Succession of the Modjadji Queens

(Source: Wikipedia extract)

1. **Rain Queen I Maselekwane Modjadji**

   (1800-1854)

2. **Rain Queen II Masalanabo Modjadji**

   (1854-1894)

3. **Rain Queen III Khetoane Modjadji**

   (1895-1959)

4. **Rain Queen IV Makoma Modjadji**

   (1959-1980)

5. **Rain Queen V Mokope Modjadji (1981-2001)**

6. Rain Queen VI Makobo Modjadji (2003-2005)

The Modern History of the Mampeules and Modjadjis

Since from the first King, every daughter would be given to Her Majestic the Queen to preserve the Royal Agreement.

As people began to be modernized and being introduced to Christianity, most of the villagers started to go to church and gradually never paid too much attention to the tradition and its significance. This lead to differences of opinions and some Royal people joined the church instead of staying true to the course of life in the royal compounds. This notion had even other Queens to deviate from the traditional way of life.

All the Modjadjis and the Mampeules are born with a great gift of Dreams. Some choose to ignore it and some stick to it. Like every other innate gift, when it is ignored, it becomes less significant to one's life. Whether you choose to ignore it or not, it doesn't go away but rather becomes less powerful.

In the late 1900's, a Zion Christian Church, became popular with the founder, known as Lekganyane, began to attract people from all over the south and the upper north of Africa. Its headquarters are just a stone throw away from the Khethlakhone Village, thus having more people moving towards the Christianity, finding a newly found church as the way to salvation.

Then Royal People who were suppose to carry on with their Royal Duties, abandoned the council and went to church.

It can be assumed that due to their innate ability to have dreams that were powerful, they were the best prophets of the church, and they helped to build it to the empire as it is today.

From the early chiefs of the Royal Council, the Mampeules have been taking care of the Royal Affairs of the Modjadji to this day, but an influence of the church has had many of them questioning the ways of the Balovhedu. The tradition is gradually getting lost in time and the modern descendents are getting on with their lives like there was never a great history of this once feared and respected powerful tribe.

The history shows in the late 1700, early 1800, the Royal Chief Council was Derrick Setene

Mampeule who met few of the White Settlers who were fascinated and rather bemused by the "nonsensical " idea that a Black Queen claims to make it rain.

The Mampeule Succession History leading to the Author

- *During the late 1700 to the early 1850's*, *Setene Mampeule* was born and he married few wives. From His First Wife, he chose a daughter who was given to the *Rain Queen II, Masalanabo Modjadji* for a wife. A son from the First wife was chosen to be the next Royal Chief Advisor to the Queen and The Royal Council.
- *During the late-1800*, *Motswalo Thomas Mampeule* was born, being the son of the Great Chief Setene Mampeule, he assumed his Chieftaincy and was sworn in after his dad's funeral. Motswalo followed and honored the great tradition and chose her daughter from the First Wife and he simply called her *Mapitshana Mampeule Modjadji,* who was offered to Her Royal Highness *the Rain Queen IV, Makoma Modjadji.* Motswalo was blessed with many children and also out of his First Wife sons; he chose one to take over from him as a Chief and advisor to the Queen.
- *In the early mid-1900*, from a great woman called *Makobo Mampeule (nee Ramathlaku)* [Motswalo's First Wife], a son was born. They named him *Molate Muller Mampeule.* Described by those who raised him and those who grew up with him, Molate showed a serious rebellious tendencies towards the traditional ways of the Balovhedu tribe. He would normally choose to opt for the highway rather than to listen to the Royal Council's way. Later he went out of the village and decided to become a police officer. It was during his training that he met his First Wife *Josephine Morohang Mahlatsi*, who was training as a nurse at Philadelphia Hospital in Mpumalanga. Together, they defied all the odds and got married regardless of what the Royal Council and Molate's father was advising against. Molate went to marry three other wives much to disapproval of the first wife which led to a nasty divorce. Morohang, begat seven children. Mpho, Thomas,(named after Motswalo), Makobo (named after Motswalo's wife), Nthabanele, Molate (Molate's junior), Masutani, and Kgotlelelo. The happy couple got separated in 1976 where Molate's wife left their Witbank home and moved back to her parents place of residence in the Free State called Heilbron, south of South Africa. Molate moved back home to Khethlakhone and joined his other wives. During this time there was no contact between him and his First wife. This is where he buried his father Motswalo and took over in 1980 as a Chief, but later abandoned the position to be the Right Hand of Bishop Lekganyane the III. In 2003, he came back to inaugurate is cousin, Her Late Royal Highness the *Rain Queen IV Makobo Modjadji* , named after Molate's mother. She lived to Rule for only two years and passed. It is rumored that Molate was approached to resume as King of the Balovhedu tribe from the initial King who ruled before he went to war only to be killed at war, but Molate refused. He also need

to appoint a successor from the First Wife's kids and offer a daughter to the Royal House., but since there is no Queen, he escapes this Royal Agreement.

The Author

COTY MAMPEULE
(*Born Kgotlelelo Martins Mampeule*)

Coty was born in a township called Witbank, Mpumalanga Region of South Africa. He is the last born of **Chief Molate Muller Mampeule** of the Balovhedu tribe and **Morohang Josephine Mampeule (maiden name, Mahlatsi)**. He was born on the 11th of January 1973.

When his parents separated in 1976, he was only 3 years old, where he moved down south with his mother and other siblings. Later he moved to a township called The Vaal, in Bophelong. This is where he stayed with his grandfather, from the mother's side. He then went to stay with his other grandmother, a sister to his mother's mother. This where in an early age, he helped her grandmother with dreams to win the Fa-Fi game of numbers. The grandmother would ask what Coty's has dreamt of and she would place the first bet of what the dream was about. Miraculously, the number would be selected and the granny would e pleased.

Later he moved with his mother to Sebokeng, then to Evaton in the late 1980's. He was later rejoined with his siblings where they all moved to Evaton Central. During that era, it was popular for grannies to ask what little kids have dreamt and would place bets with such dream results. He was recognized by few women in the yard they used to share and would ask what his dream was and they would come back smiling.

In 1981 he started his schooling in a primary school called Montsosi under a strict Head Mistress called Connie Mbowani. He excelled in his studies but prone to sicknesses all the time. He contracted pneumonia that nearly caused him his life. He then finished his primary and went to a higher primary called Phepane High under Mr. Mphahlele. He received a bursary for the Best Academic Student in Grade 8's.

He then tried to move back to his birthplace in Witbank but came to The Vaal. He joined a secondary school called Tokelo High and finished his Matric in 1991. He then went to further his studies at Vaal University of Technology, where studied BCommerce degree where he concentrated in Business Management, Economics and Accounting Sciences.

He then joined the First National Bank for his first professional employment. And then moved to SABMiller Group where he continued to work as a Sales person. Then he joined All-pay Group (ABSA Subsidiary) and he worked with Government Grant Payments.

He later joined Pernod Ricard South Africa under David de Mardt, as a Sales Representative, and later got promoted to a Manager is Sales. He later was promoted to Activations and Promotions.

He then joined a South African based company called The Ceres Beverages Company a s a Divisional Activations Manager. Then he formed his own company and sees to its daily survival.

His interest in LOTTO & DREAMS started in 2000 when LOTTO was introduced to South African Public, and he became more and more vivid as he would give people his Dreams and they would come back with mismatched but correct numbers. He then studied the Fa-Fi system which never even had a base where he can start working.

In gradual years he perfected his research and came to notice that DREAMS played an important role in the games of chance. He then found a way to systematize his work and finally decided to share his work and methods by creating a blog where he uses to help and interprets the International Lotteries Results by converting them into Dreams and vice versa. The Fanatic LOTTO and POWER-BALL players will find this book, a revelation to DREAMS MYSTERIES and the Game Of Chance.

We hope you enjoy the book.

Thanking you Sincerely...

Vote of Thanks

To Pasi Makobo Mampeule:

Thank you for believing in me, you have helped me to believe in myself.

To my late Granny Mampoti Sobane:

I know you are teaching Angels how to Love.

To Refiloe:

I still love you for all kinds of good reasons.

To my Aunty Her Majesty the Royal Wife

Mapitshana Modjadji-Mampeule:

I simply thank God for you.

To my mom and dad:

You guys rock my world.

To all who have bought this ebook?

Be so kind to pass on the Great News...

I love you all!!!